I0555265

Mind Over
ANXIETY

Using
Mindfulness & Meditation
to Rewire Your Brain
and Conquer Stress

Brian Luke Seaward, PhD

WETWARE MEDIA

Publisher's Note

This publication offers informational content on its subject matter but does not constitute professional advice in psychology, finance, law, or other specialized areas. Readers requiring expert guidance should consult a qualified professional.

Copyright ©2025 by Brian Luke Seaward
All Rights Reserved

Wetware Media, LLC
wetwaremedia.com

Cover design by Faradila Sofiani
Edited by Connie Shaw

ISBN: 978-1-954566-08-8

Publisher's Cataloging-in-Publication Data

Names: Seaward, Brian Luke, author.
Title: Mind over anxiety : using mindfulness and meditation to rewire your brain and conquer stress / Brian Luke Seaward, PhD.
Description: Boulder, CO: Wetware Media, 2025.
Identifiers: LCCN: 2025946520 | ISBN: 978-1-954566-08-8
Subjects: LCSH Meditation--Therapeutic use. | Mindfulness (Psychology) | Mindfulness-based cognitive therapy. | Stress management. | Stress (Psychology) | BISAC SELF-HELP / Self-Management / Stress Management | BODY, MIND & SPIRIT / Mindfulness & Meditation
Classification: LCC RA785 .S434 2025 | DDC 155.9042--dc23

Praise for *Mind Over Anxiety*

"Dr. Brian Luke Seaward shares proven strategies and practical tools that will help you maintain calm amid life's storms. This is more than a book — it's a manual for living well. In a time when more people are facing chronic anxiety, we have never needed his wisdom more."

– **Heidi Hanna**, *NY Times* best-selling author, *The Sharp Solution: A Brain-Based Approach for Optional Performance, and Stressaholic*

"Dr. Brian Luke Seaward offers a wise, compassionate, and practical guide for anyone seeking calm in the midst of life's turbulence. *Mind Over Anxiety* provides tools that are both accessible and transformative. It is not only a roadmap for easing stress, but also a companion for self-discovery and living from love rather than fear."

– **Mark Lersch**, MA, LPC, Boulder, CO

"Stress and anxiety affect us all to varying depths. Many approaches to relieve these have been proposed, including rigid "You MUST Relax" efforts that likely INCREASE stress! Dr. Brian Luke Seaward provides an adaptive and flexible approach that has provided benefits to our coworkers, patients, and their families."

– **Richard R. Riker** MD, FCCM, Neuroscientist and Sedation Researcher

"I've known Dr. Brian Luke Seaward for over 35 years, and his guidance helped me stay calm, focused, and resilient while training for the Olympics. *Mind Over Anxiety* gives you the same tools to conquer stress, rewire your brain, and thrive in every area of life. It is a rare gem—practical, powerful, and transformative."

– **Sergio Lopez Miro**, Two-time Olympic medalist and five-time Olympic coach

"Clear, practical, and timely! This book makes mindfulness and meditation approachable at a time when we need them most. Blending brain science with everyday tips, it shows not just why these practices matter, but also how to find calm and clarity in the midst of chaotic times."

– **Donna L. Hamilton**, MD, MS, Trauma Informed Well-being strategist & coach

Also by Brian Luke Seaward

Managing Stress 11e
Managing Stress: A Creative Journal (4e)
Health and Wellness Journal Workbook (2e)
Managing Stress in Emergency Medical Services
Achieving the Mind-Body-Spirit Connection
Stand Like Mountain, Flow Like Water: Reflections on Stress
and Human Spirituality
Table for Two, Please
Essentials of Managing Stress 5e
Health of the Human Spirit (2e)
Stressed Is Desserts Spelled Backward (revised edition)
Quiet Mind, Fearless Heart: A Taoist Path Through Stress and
Spirituality
The Art of Calm: Relaxation Through the Five Senses
Hot Stones & Funny Bones
The Art of Peace and Relaxation Workbook
Essentials of Managing Stress During Times of Pandemic
The Road to Wellness
A Good Night's Sleep
The Doors of Perception Wisdom Pack
A Beautiful World
A Return to Ireland
Hummingbirds: Crown Jewels of the Bird World
Triumph of the Human Spirit: 52 Soul-searching Journal
Exercises for Personal Resiliency

Audio
Above the Fray
NatureScapes
Sweet Surrender
A Wing & A Prayer
A Change of Heart

Dedication

Thank you to all my former college students, and the Olympic athletes, military personnel, corporate executives, and thousands of workshop and retreat participants from Maine to Colorado, from Hawaii to California, who have practiced these skills of mindfulness and inner peace to make the world a better place.

Contents

Preface

Important Note to the Reader

While the mindfulness and meditation techniques presented in this book can be valuable tools for managing stress and anxiety, they are not a substitute for professional medical or mental health care. If you are experiencing severe anxiety, depression, or other mental health concerns, I strongly recommend you work with a licensed therapist or mental health professional, particularly one experienced with mindfulness-based approaches.

Do not discontinue or alter any prescribed medications without first consulting your physician or psychiatrist. If you are currently in treatment, please discuss these practices with your healthcare provider to ensure they complement your existing care plan.

My Story

Like too many children of my generation, I grew up in a household of two abusive, alcoholic parents. Anxiety wasn't just a concept; it was an everyday fact of a very fear-based life. During the many turbulent years of childhood and throughout my teenage years, however, I had periods of tremendous calm and resilience. Wandering through the forest beyond my backyard became a regular mindfulness meditation practice long before I ever heard the term "mindfulness." Whether through luck or divine intervention, I was guided into moments of calm and solitude that I quickly learned to integrate for mind-body-spirit balance. Personally, I found meditation to be an invaluable tool for staying grounded and centered in times of change and uncertainty. It is a practice that I have used ever since.

Many people are aware of Olympic champion Michael Phelps, but before him, there was an Olympic champion named

Mark Spitz. Spitz became my personal hero when I needed a positive role model, and through competitive swimming, I learned mental training, which certainly includes meditation. In athletics, mindfulness is called "being in the flow," and my meditation practice was an asset to my competitive swimming career and, later, my long-distance running practice. Today, my meditation practice includes an hour-long mindfulness walk in a nature preserve each morning, followed by a thirty-minute energy breath work practice before breakfast. It's a great way to start each day.

In 1983, I was invited to be the sports psychologist for the Olympic Biathlon team for the Calgary Games in Canada, and then again for some Olympic swimmers and ice skaters in the 1992 games. I introduced our team members to the practice of meditation as a means to reduce competitive anxiety and improve performance, and it worked wonders.

For the past forty-five years I have been teaching stress management from a mind-body-spirit perspective. In addition to addressing the symptoms of stress (e.g., muscle tension, chronic illness, etc.), this holistic approach places a focus on the integration, balance and harmony of mind, body, spirit, and emotions, and emphasizes love and compassion. Meditation, in all its many forms, is a powerful tool for just this purpose. Moving through our lives from a motivation of love and compassion instead of fear and anger is how we reach our highest potential.

Today, the world is filled with great angst and uncertainty, with repeated gusts of turbulent change. I am delighted to share the timeless wisdom of meditation with you to help keep you grounded and centered and provide a sense of balance in your lives. May these skills work wonders in your life as they have for so many of my students, colleagues, and friends.

Introduction

"Inside the chaos, build a temple of love."
—Rumi

In today's fast-paced world, anxiety has become an unwelcome companion for many of us, quietly eroding our sense of peace and well-being. Yet, what if I told you that the same techniques used by world-class athletes, celebrated artists, and successful business leaders could help you find balance in your daily life?

Consider this: Taylor Swift, Kobe Bryant, Selena Gomez, Novak Djokovic, Lady Gaga, and even U.S. Navy SEALs all share a powerful secret—they meditate and practice mindfulness. These high performers have discovered what ancient wisdom has long taught us: that mindfulness and meditation are not merely spiritual practices, but essential tools for maintaining mental clarity, emotional stability, and personal resilience in our demanding world.

Let me share a compelling story that illustrates the transformative power of focused attention. In 1973, tennis legend Billie Jean King faced Bobby Riggs in the famous "Battle of the Sexes" match. While Riggs, a self-proclaimed male chauvinist, approached the match with arrogance and minimal preparation, King understood that victory would require more than physical prowess—it demanded extraordinary mental strength. Her preparation included an ingenious form of meditation: she would place a tennis ball atop her television and focus on it while her favorite shows played below, training herself to maintain concentration amidst distraction. This dedication to mental training contributed to her historic victory, demonstrating how meditation techniques can be adapted to overcome life's challenges.

In this book, we'll explore practical strategies for managing anxiety and stress through four comprehensive sections:

1. Brain Basics: Understanding the fundamental workings of your mind

2. Meditation and Mindfulness Foundations: Learning the essential principles

3. Techniques for Anxiety and Stress Management: Building your toolkit

4. Cultivating Calm: Guided Practices for Lasting Peace

The mind-body-spirit connection is more than just a concept—it's a scientifically validated framework for better living. Current research confirms what practitioners have known for millennia: regular meditation can enhance sleep quality, strengthen immune function, improve mental health, and build emotional resilience. These benefits aren't just for elite athletes or spiritual masters; they're accessible to anyone willing to learn and practice.

As someone who has spent decades teaching stress management and resilience to Olympic athletes, corporate executives, healthcare professionals, military personnel, and others, I've witnessed firsthand how these techniques can transform lives. Drawing from my experience as a health psychologist and resiliency coach, as well as information from numerous books I've written on stress management, I'll share proven strategies that combine ancient wisdom with modern science.

In the pages that follow, we'll not only explore the fundamentals of stress and anxiety management but also tackle contemporary challenges like digital toxicity. You'll learn practical techniques for breathing, body awareness, and meditation that can help you maintain calm amid life's storms.

This isn't just another self-help book—it's a practical guide to reclaiming your peace of mind in an increasingly chaotic world. Whether you're dealing with daily stress, competitive pressure, or chronic anxiety, the techniques in this book can help you develop the mental strength and emotional resilience to thrive in these unprecedented times of both personal and planetary challenges.

Are you ready to begin your journey toward a calmer, more balanced life? Let's take the first step together.

PART ONE

Brain Basics

"The idea that the brain can change its own structure and function through thought and activity is, I believe, the most important alteration in our view of the brain since we first sketched out its basic anatomy and the workings of its basic component, the neuron."

— Norman Doidge

1

Anxiety and the Brain: Unpacking the Science

Let's take a short journey through the human brain and learn how it relates to anxiety and meditation. As we navigate the complexities of the mind, we'll discover how our understanding of this remarkable organ has evolved over time. Before we delve into current perspectives and cutting-edge research, though, it's crucial to appreciate the groundwork laid by earlier scientists, researchers, and thinkers. This historical context will not only deepen our appreciation for the field but also help us grasp the monumental strides we've made in our knowledge of the brain. From early theories to modern neuroscience, each discovery has built upon the last, leading us to our current understanding of the brain's incredible plasticity and its potential for change.

Navigating the Chaos of Modern Life

This evolving knowledge couldn't be more relevant as we progress through the 21st century, where life seems to be moving at an ever-increasing pace. Our growing understanding of the brain's adaptability is crucial in an era when we're constantly challenged by the rapid flow of information and stimuli around us. We're bombarded with sensory stimulation from all directions, much of it from social media and technology. Don't get me wrong—technology isn't inherently bad, but how we use (or misuse) it can be problematic.

As we navigate this high-speed world, we're draining our energy through incessant stimulation, and this can leave us feeling depleted, overwhelmed, confused and anxious. Practices that help us slow down and recharge become increasingly crucial for our mental and emotional well-being. Meditation has emerged as a powerful tool to counteract the effects of our fast-paced lifestyle. It offers a respite from the endless stream of stimuli, providing a great way to restore your personal energy and replenish your inner well. By carving out time for stillness and reflection, we can cultivate resilience and maintain balance amidst the chaos of modern life.

Calm is Your Superpower

I love the idea that "calm is your superpower." It's a superpower that is inherent, yet dormant in most of us. The power of calm is really the underlying message here—how to regain a sense of calm in our chaotic world and claim it as your superpower. When we say this, we acknowledge the strength of maintaining composure and clarity in the face of chaos. It's about developing the ability to pause, breathe, and respond intentionally, rather than react impulsively to the stressors around us, to cultivate an inner stillness that allows us to engage with life more effectively. By mastering this superpower, we can navigate life's challenges with greater ease and resilience, transforming our experience of the world around us. To fully appreciate this superpower and understand how the mind works to provide a sense of calm, a refresher about the dynamics of the brain helps.

Pioneers of Brain Research

One of my heroes in the field of brain research is Richard Davidson from the University of Wisconsin-Madison. He's renowned for his work measuring Buddhist monks during meditation using Magnetic Resonance Imaging (MRIs) and functional Magnetic Resonance Imaging (fMRIs), and he significantly contributed to popularizing the term "neuroplasticity" in the American lexicon.

Before MRIs, the best way to research brain mechanics was through EEGs—electroencephalography. You might have seen people in movies with electrodes attached to their heads—that's EEG. This technology helped us identify different states of consciousness associated with various brainwave patterns like Beta, Alpha, Theta, and Delta. Interestingly, Alpha and Theta waves are particularly prevalent during meditation.

Let me introduce you to someone who truly revolutionized our understanding of the brain by building on the foundation of such pioneering work: Roger Sperry. His "split-brain" research won him a Nobel Prize in 1981 and gave us the concepts of left-brain and right-brain thinking.

Sperry worked with four patients who had severe epilepsy. In an effort to reduce the intensity and frequency of their Grand Mal seizures, he severed the corpus callosum—the bridge between the left and right hemispheres—with tremendous success! To his astonishment, this also led to useful observations and a better understanding of how the two hemispheres function, revealing surprisingly distinct differences. Today, we know that the brain's functioning involves significantly more complexity than the cerebral roles of the left and right hemispheres, however, this ground-breaking research laid a solid foundation for understanding the mysteries of consciousness and the brain.

Understanding the Brain's Structure and Function

To further explore how the brain can adapt and change, it's important to understand its basic systems. Don't worry, we're not aiming for a Ph.D. here, just the essentials.

You may remember from anatomy and physiology that the brain has three levels: the brainstem (including the spinal cord), the limbic system (which controls fight-or-flight responses), and the neocortex (responsible for higher consciousness and cognition).

Here's an interesting fact: the brain has over 85 billion highly interconnected neurons, constantly self-organizing into systems for emotions, feelings, cognition, memory, and self-control. Neurons are grouped into different regions for various functions, which are influenced by activities like meditation.

COHERENCE: MAKING TWO BRAINS WHOLE!

One of the more common ways to determine brain activity during stress is to attach electrodes to the scalp and observe brain wave activity (e.g., Alpha, Beta, Delta and Theta waves). Under stress, the left hemisphere of the brain (associated with judgement, analysis, logic, and time awareness) appears to be more active (more Beta waves). When the hemispheres of the brain are not in sync, there is said to be a lack of coherence. Studies conducted to determine the effects of meditation on brain waves reveal that during meditation, there is greater coherence between the left and right hemispheres of the brain and higher Alpha power (relaxation) in the frontal cortex. Coherence means harmonious order and efficient use of energy. Simply stated: Coherence between the left and right cerebral hemispheres indicates a more grounded, unified effort of consciousness to effectively deal with the stress of life.

Researchers, including those at the HeartMath Institute, have also investigated heart and brain coherence to reveal that a regular meditation practice promotes greater feelings of wholeness, decreased stress, enhanced creativity, greater resilience, greater emotional composure and improved physical health. When the heart and mind are aligned, mind, body and spirit benefit greatly, and we can become our best selves.

In addition to the left and right cerebral hemispheres, several key brain regions include the prefrontal cortex (responsible for working memory and executive decision-making), the amygdala (part of the limbic system, associated with the fight-or-flight response), the hippocampus (involved in memory, learning, and emotions), the thalamus (an information relay station), the hypothalamus (managing the autonomic nervous system and regulating hormones), the nucleus accumbens (linking motivation and action), the occipital cortex (related to vision), and the pineal gland (regulating circadian rhythms and melatonin production).

The Brain's Remarkable Plasticity

The fact that all these brain regions can be affected by our thoughts and activities, such as meditation, helps coordinate brain functions for optimal performance in thought processes (e.g., creativity, pattern recognition, judgment, intuition, curiosity, etc.), memory, and reaction time. The brain is arguably the most important and certainly the most complex organ in the body, and despite our growing comprehension of its workings, it remains less understood than other organs like the heart, liver, and kidneys. Its complexity surpasses that of any computer we can imagine.

Now, here's something crucial to understand: the brain's anatomy isn't fixed by age twenty. That's a myth! Brain tissue is dynamic and flexible—hence the term "neuroplasticity." This means that neurons aren't fixed in number or position; they're constantly changing, forming new connections, and even generating new neurons in response to our experiences and environment. This plasticity allows us to learn new skills, recover from injuries, and adapt to new situations throughout our lives. It's a fundamental quality that underpins our ability to grow and change, both mentally and emotionally, well into old age.

This understanding has revolutionized brain research. We now know that the brain can recover remarkably from trauma and strokes, even stress in the form of PTSD (post-traumatic stress disorder). People who have lost the ability to speak or to control their movements have, in some cases, regained these faculties. It's truly amazing.

There's a wonderful expression: "neurons that fire together, wire together." This means that when neurons are activated simultaneously, they form stronger connections, allowing us to learn new tasks and skills at any age. But here's the caveat: these changes need to be reinforced through repeated behavior, and without repetition, the connections may weaken and fade over time. It's like the old joke—"How do you get to Carnegie Hall? Practice, practice, practice!"

This idea ties into two important processes in the brain: neurogenesis (the creation of new neurons) and synaptic pruning (the removal of unused connections). Both processes are influenced by our repeated feelings, behaviors, and activities like exercise and meditation, that can help sculpt the brain's structure and functioning over time to support mental agility and emotional well-being.

Think of it this way: When you're learning a new skill, it's like driving on a bumpy dirt road. The more you practice, the smoother that road becomes, eventually turning into a superhighway. Here's the great news: The process of neuroplasticity can occur in a few as seven days. Meditating for seven days begins the rewiring process for relaxation, calm and inner peace.

Exploring the Mystery of Consciousness

While the brain is often likened to an incredible organic computer, the mind poses a deeper mystery. Consciousness is often referred to by Western scientists as an "epiphenomenon of the brain" or "the ghost in the machine," highlighting the perplexing relationship between our physical brain functions and our subjective experience of thoughts, emotions, premonitions, intuition, intention, and awareness. This duality of mind and brain prompts profound questions about the nature of existence and the essence of human experience.

Just as scientists have explored the dynamics of brain structure and function, so too have renowned researchers, including Carl

Jung, Wilder Penfield, Robert Ornstein, Elmer Green, Charles Tart, Beverly Rubik, Joe Dispenza, Robert Monroe, Bruce Lipton and Dean Radin, explored many aspects of the conscious and unconscious mind, with some remarkable findings. Simply stated, the mind is a form of conscious energy that uses the brain as its primary organ to sense and interpret the world we live in.

So, what is the mind? It's a very complex question without a simple answer, largely because it encompasses interconnected aspects of human experience—such as thoughts, emotions, intuition, pre-cognition, perceptions, and consciousness—that are subjective and not easily quantifiable. Knowing this, the question arises, how does stress impact consciousness in daily life? What is consciousness in terms of daily functioning? Perhaps most importantly, how can we harness the power of the mind to achieve our highest potential, rather than sabotaging it's best efforts when faced repeatedly with daily challenges and life-pressing issues? One of the skills developed in this book is how to harness the power of your mind's potential and not let stressful thoughts live "rent-free" in your head.

Consciousness encompasses abilities such as deciding to buy something, figuring out the appropriate thing to say to a friend or colleague, and remembering where you last placed your cell phone. It includes information processing, problem-solving, memory recall, decision making, reaction time, and pattern recognition, an essential aptitude for a baby to recognize familiar faces like her parents'. Critical thinking skills, intuition and memory are vital components, guiding how we assess security and interpret our surroundings.

Meditation, notably, affects all these facets of consciousness.

2

What Is Neuroplasticity? Can You Really "Rewire" Your Brain?

You've probably heard people say "It's all in your head"—and they're not entirely wrong! What's going on in the space between our ears is absolutely fascinating, and it's time we took a closer look at this remarkable organ we call the human brain.

The Basic Blueprint: Your Brain's Architecture

Before we dive into the magic of neuroplasticity, let's get our bearings with some brain basics. Don't worry—we won't get too technical. Think of your brain as a three-story building:

Ground Floor: brainstem and spinal cord

Second Floor: limbic system (your emotional center and home of the fight-or-flight response)

Penthouse Suite: neocortex (our uniquely human level of higher consciousness)

Here's a fun fact that might come in handy if you ever end up on the TV show *Jeopardy!* Your brain contains over 85 billion neurons, all constantly organizing themselves into five main aspects: emotions, feelings, cognition (awareness), memory, and self-control. That's more complex than any computer ever built!

Meet Your Brain's Key Players

Let's introduce you to some important parts of your brain—think of them as the main characters in our story:

Prefrontal Cortex: your brain's CEO, sitting right behind your forehead, handling executive decisions and working memory

Amygdala: your security system, always on alert for potential threats

Hippocampus: your internal librarian, filing away memories and helping you learn

Thalamus and Hypothalamus: your message center and body manager, respectively

Nucleus Accumbens: your motivation-to-action converter

Occipital Cortex: your visual processing center

Pineal Gland: Your internal clock, keeping your daily rhythms in check

Stress: The Brain's Biggest Challenge

Here's something crucial to understand: stress isn't just "all in your head"—it's a full-body experience that can either help or hinder your brain's amazing neuroplasticity. When stress hits (whether it's real or imagined), your brain kicks into fight-or-flight action (survival mode) like a well-oiled machine:

1. The hypothalamus sounds the alarm: *Danger!*

2. The pituitary gland (your body's master control center) springs into action.

3. Your adrenal glands release a cocktail of stress hormones for physical survival.

This response is invaluable if you're running from a bear or mountain lion, but not so helpful—in fact, it's a huge liability—when you're trying to make important decisions, learn new skills, or communicate effectively. That's why experts say never to make big decisions when you're stressed—your brain is compromised and literally isn't working at its best! Here is a fact that should be headline news: The body doesn't know the difference between an actual threat (e.g., the house is on fire), or a manufactured threat (e.g., embarrassment at a dinner party) created by ego-based thoughts. The body's stress alarm responds the same way.

Stress and Neuroplasticity

We now know that repeated episodes of stress can indeed affect both the structure and function of brain physiology. For instance, repeated stress hormonal activity can shrink (atrophy) the pre-frontal cortex (where sound decisions are made) and enlarge (hypertrophy) the amygdala, where the stress alarm is triggered. Researchers now see this same rewiring occurring (with an accompanying dose of dopamine) through repeated social media doom-scrolling and fear-based click-bait screen use. In essence, repeated stressful perceptions can rewire the brain to engage in the stress response more quickly, making it harder to achieve a state of calm and inner peace.

The Stress-Anxiety Connection

It's worth noting that stress and anxiety, while related, are different beasts:

Stress is like your brain's radar system picking up external threats.

Anxiety is more like your brain's alarm system getting stuck in the "on" position.

Stress is a natural part of life, as you make sense of your environment so you can feel safe and secure. Anxiety is a perpetual state of fear, which is not natural.

Understanding this difference can help you better manage both conditions and support your brain's natural ability to adapt and grow.

Rewiring Your Brain: The Science of Change

Remember that the neuroplasticity of the brain means that you can continue to learn throughout your life because your brain can rewire itself to accommodate new information. And here's something you may not know: when you're having fun while learning, your brain creates new connections much faster. While it typically takes about forty repetitions to create a new synapse, this drops to just ten to twelve repetitions when you're in a playful, relaxed state. Talk about a shortcut!

Meditation: Your Brain's Gym Membership

Want to hear something amazing about meditation? In as little as seven days of regular practice, scientists can actually see changes happening in the brain. But the real magic happens around the eight-week mark. Here's what you can expect:

Week 1: Your neurons start forming new connections (think of walking on a dirt path).

Week 2-7: With each practice, the path becomes more worn and easier to travel.

By week 8: You'll likely notice yourself feeling more present and focused, less anxious, and more comfortable, perhaps even happier.

In his acclaimed book, *10% Happier*, former network news journalist Dan Harris found that engaging in a regular meditation practice gave him a greater sense of calm and happiness. He admits that most likely it's more than 10%, but this is a good starting point. A more accessible state of happiness is just one benefit; there are many more. In fact, the benefits of a regular meditation practice are amazing!

The long-term benefits include:

- Sharper focus and attention span (clear thinking)
- Better emotional control (things roll off your back)
- Improved memory (short term and long term)
- Faster reaction time
- Enhanced problem-solving skills
- Stronger intuition
- Deeper sense of awe and appreciation
- Better quality sleep

The Daily Construction Work: Neurogenesis

Here's another amazing fact: your brain is creating new neurons every single day through a process called "neurogenesis." Think of it as your brain's construction crew, building new neural pathways, based on what you do repeatedly. But there's also a cleanup crew at work; through something called synaptic pruning, your brain removes connections you're not using anymore.

Your Brain's Remarkable Recovery Powers

The invention of the MRI machine opened up a whole new world of brain research. We've witnessed remarkable recoveries— people regaining speech after strokes, relearning motor control, even rewiring their brains to work around damaged areas. It's like your brain is the ultimate adaptation machine, constantly reorganizing itself to meet new challenges.

The Key to Change: Practice Makes Permanent

Here's the really exciting part: you can literally reshape your brain through repeated practice. Whether you're learning to meditate, mastering a new skill, picking up a new language, or working to overcome a challenge, your brain will adapt to meet the demands you place on it. Both at the microscopic level of individual neurons and the macro level of entire brain regions, change happens through consistent practice.

Remember: Rome wasn't built in a day, and neither is a calmer, more focused mind. The changes happening in your brain might be gradual, but they're profound. Trust the process, keep practicing, and know that every small step you take is reshaping your brain for the better.

The take-home message? Your brain is incredibly adaptable, constantly changing, and ready to help you learn new things at any age. All you need to do is give it the right kind of exercise, manage your stress levels, and practice consistently. So, the next time someone tells you "You can't teach an old dog new tricks," you can tell them about neuroplasticity and how science has proven that it's never too late to learn, grow, and change.

Optimizing Your Brain's Health

Enhanced neuroplasticity through meditation practice for a sounder conscious mind is wonderful; however, this alone is not enough to maintain a healthy brain. There are other things you can do to optimize the function of these neural pathways among the gray matter of your brain to help achieve your highest potential. The following are all commonsense behaviors but they bear repeating in the context of mind over anxiety

1. Get a good night's sleep. Seven to eight hours is essential for physiological rest. Less than seven hours is not enough time to remove waste products that, when left residing in your brain tissue, decrease memory.

2. Maintain a healthy diet. A balanced intake of Omega 3 and 6 oils helps to decrease inflammation. Avoid food chemicals (neurotoxins) that cross the blood-brain barrier and compromise thought processing. Minimize simple sugars that cause inflammation.

3. Decrease screen time, particularly one to two hours before bedtime.

4. Get out in nature daily. Our circadian rhythms get recalibrated with natural sunlight.

5. Engage in regular cardio exercise (3 x week). Some studies show that exercise is the best stimulator for neurogenesis.

FUN FACTS ABOUT THE BRAIN

- The brain weighs about three pounds.
- The brain is comprised of over eighty-five billion neurons.
- Neurons are grouped into different regions of the brain for distinct functions.
- There are trillions of synaptic connections participating in an ongoing process throughout life.

Practice Digital Hygiene, Avoid Digital Toxicity

While we are on the subject of brain health, let's revisit the topic of digital hygiene. FOMO (fear of missing out) is a stress-prone attitude that can promote and maintain feelings of anxiety. Research now reveals that screen behaviors that include hours on social media (particularly doom scrolling) and engaging in click-baiting activities train the mind to engage in what is called hyper-vigilance, a common symptom of PTSD. In essence, these kinds of behavior wire the brain for stress, thus the need for the concepts digital toxicity and digital detox. Experts suggest turning off the computer screen two hours before bedtime so that your mind is not racing before your head hits the pillow. Moreover, researchers note that light from screen devices compromises the pineal gland's ability to produce melatonin (a necessary neurochemical to promote sleep)—another reason for no screen use before bed. Additionally, spending hours of time online at any time of the day does not give the mind a chance to rest and properly process information, specifically to store short term memory bits of information into longer memory. Despite its tendency to lead to digital toxicity and screen addictions, please keep in mind that technology itself is not bad; we just need strong, healthy boundaries for its use. Do you have healthy boundaries with your screen devices? Now is the time to create and implement them (see Appendix A).

PART TWO

Meditation and Mindfulness Foundations

"Meditation helps me to transcend and get beyond the grip of all the negativity and regenerate from within a more positive attitude.."

— Mike Love, The Beach Boys

3

Mindfulness and Meditation: Powerful Tools for Transformation

There's an ancient saying, "When the pupil is ready, the teacher will come." This wisdom suggests that a calm mind can access deep inner knowledge. In our fast-paced world of constant distractions, the need for such mental clarity has never been greater. This explains the recent surge in popularity of meditation and mindfulness, ancient practices that offer respite from modern sensory overload. These techniques teach us to observe our thoughts objectively, respond thoughtfully to stress, and find moments of peace amid chaos. By cultivating a non-judgmental awareness of our mental states, we learn to step back from the whirlwind of our thoughts and emotions, creating space for more deliberate and balanced responses to life's challenges.

The Marathon Lesson: Focusing on the Finish Line

I've worked with many Olympic athletes, so many of my insights about mental training and mindfulness first came from the world of athletics. One particularly poignant story involves Greta Waitz, a marathon runner who medaled in the Olympics and won several Boston Marathon titles in the 1980s and 1990s. The Boston Marathon, a grueling 26-mile race that takes about two and a half hours to complete, provided a valuable lesson in focus for Waitz. In her first few competitions, as she ran, spectators would call out her name in encouragement. Initially, she would turn her head to acknowledge them, but she quickly realized that this small action was costing her precious time. Over the course of the marathon, these tiny movements added up to several minutes lost.

Waitz learned that to win, she needed to stay focused, minimize distractions, and keep her eyes focused on the finish line. Despite thousands of people cheering for her, she maintained her attention, aways looking straight ahead. Some spectators initially thought she was being rude, but Waitz understood that those cheers, as well-intentioned as they were, served as distractions from her ultimate goal: a victorious first place finish. This story beautifully illustrates the importance of focus from distractions in our daily lives.

The Necessity of Mindfulness in a Distracted World

Meditation and mindfulness are powerful tools for health, wellbeing, and personal transformation. They're essential components of self-care, helping us build resilience in the face of life's challenges. But why are these practices so crucial in today's world? We live in an age of sensory bombardment, constantly inundated with scores of bits and bytes of information. While this connectivity can be beneficial, there comes a point when it becomes overwhelming (an apt metaphor is drinking from a fire hydrant and being knocked over). The consequences of this sensory overload are manifold: burnout, frustration and anger, difficulty concentrating, apathy, and rising rates of anxiety and depression.

What is Meditation?

At its core, meditation is a proven means to decrease sensory bombardment, helping us regain a sense of mental homeostasis. Meditation also helps decrease the internal distractions promoted by the ego. By intentionally focusing our attention and creating a buffer against external stimuli and as internal distractions, this practice allows our overloaded nervous system to reset and recalibrate. This cultivates a state of inner calm and balance that extends beyond the meditation session, enabling us to navigate life's challenges with greater clarity and composure. The goal of meditation isn't to control your thoughts. Rather, the purpose of meditation is to stop letting your thoughts control you!

FUN FACTS ABOUT THE EGO

- The ego is an abstract concept popularized by Sigmond Freud.
- The ego goes by other names including the lower self, the shadow, ego-mind and anatta.
- The ego is associated with vanity, arrogance, narcissism and insecurity, but also self-esteem.
- The purpose of the ego is to avoid pain and promote pleasure (according to Freud).
- It is the ego that trips the fight (anger) or flight (fear) response when it detects danger.
- To minimize pain the ego uses defense mechanisms (e.g. denial, projection, rationalization).
- The ego is a great bodyguard, but a lousy CEO.
- It's the ego that exaggerates emotional responses, in essence "hijacking" one's emotional reactions and creating emotional control dramas.
- Meditation helps calm ego-based or fear-based thoughts long enough to access wisdom from the unconscious mind, hence the expression "when the student is ready the teacher will come."

Domesticate the Ego

Even if there were no distractions like cell phones or binge screen watching, the ego part of the mind has no problem creating an abundance of distractions itself, often far more alarming than those from the external world. Thoughts, perceptions, opinions, and memories can surface immediately to steal our attention from the most important of all thought processes. For this reason, meditation experts from long ago described meditation as "domesticating the ego." Remember: the ego itself is not bad; it is primarily our bodyguard. However, it is not ever supposed to be CEO. Meditation is a means to put the ego back in its proper job responsibility, for if this doesn't happen, there will be "emotional poop" everywhere. Sages and wisdom keepers from all corners of the globe remind us to domesticate the ego daily.

Remember, You Are Not Your Thoughts

Meditation, in all its many forms, reminds us to stop, pause and observe. Observe the present moment, your breathing, your thoughts, your emotions. Don't judge any of these; simply observe! One of the most important concepts in meditation is to understand that you are not your thoughts. When you can learn to observe your thoughts and feelings, you begin to realize the observer is not creating these thoughts, it merely recognizes and acknowledges them. There is great power in observation. There is great discipline in observation. There is great calm in observation.

Taming the "Monkey Mind"

The importance of strengthening our focusing skills through meditation becomes even more apparent when we consider recent studies showing that our attention spans have shortened dramatically. Some even claim we now have shorter attention spans than goldfish! This alarming trend underscores the need for practices that help us regain control of our wandering minds.

In our digital age, where notifications, alerts, and pings, all with urgent information, constantly vie for our attention, the ability to sustain focus has become a valuable skill. "Monkey mind" is a term used to describe a wandering or distracted mind full of thoughts ricocheting all over the place. If the monkey metaphor doesn't work for you, think squirrel! Avoid "squirrel mind."

FUN FACTS ABOUT THE MIND

- The mind is considered an abstract concept, often described through metaphor.
- A popular metaphor, popularized by Carl Jung, is an iceberg floating in an ocean of water.
- The mind is often divided into sections: the conscious mind above the water, the subconscious right below the water, and the unconscious way below the water.
- Experts suggest only 10% of the mind is conscious (above the water) with 90% subconscious and unconscious (below the water).
- Experts also suggest that it is the unconscious mind that governs behavior.
- The ego acts as the censor between the conscious and subconscious minds.
- The unconscious mind speaks in the language of symbols, metaphors, colors and dream fragments, whereas the conscious mind uses primarily words.
- Meditation helps lower the water level to make the unconscious rise to consciousness.

When Should You Not Meditate?

Don't meditate after you've had a large meal; you'll likely fall asleep. There's a physiological dynamic called "postprandial lethargy." If you end up on Jeopardy, you might need to know that! It means if you eat a big meal, a lot of blood stays in your stomach to digest the food, and with less blood traveling to your head, you won't have the ideal amount of oxygen to stay awake. Also, if you're feeling really tired and drained, physically ill, or emotionally raw, it might be better to rest, take a walk, or calm down first, then revisit your meditation practice later in the day or evening.

Meditation as a Way of Life

This enhanced focus enriches our overall quality of life beyond mere productivity gains. By learning to be fully present, we derive greater satisfaction from our experiences, whether savoring a tasty meal, truly listening to a friend, or immersing ourselves in creative work. This mindful approach breaks the cycle of constant distractions and multitasking that often leaves us feeling scattered, unfulfilled, even anxious. These essential skills developed through a regular meditation practice serve as a powerful tool for maintaining mental and emotional balance in our chaotic world, allowing us to respond to challenges with clarity and composure rather than reacting on autopilot. Thus, meditation evolves from a simple daily practice into a way of life, enabling us to fully engage with the world while maintaining inner calm and focus, ultimately leading to a richer, more balanced existence.

4

Benefits of
Mindfulness and Meditation

Let me share something that might surprise you: meditation and mindfulness are terms that are often used interchangeably; however, they aren't the same thing. More like close cousins than twins, both styles of mental training help you find peace, just in slightly different ways. After forty-five years of studying stress management, I've seen both practices transform lives, and I'm excited to tell you why.

The Magic of Meditation

Picture this: see and sense yourself sitting by a peaceful mountain stream. That's what meditation can feel like once you get the hang of it. It's your daily mini-vacation from the chaos of life, a chance to step back, catch your breath and just be. When you meditate, you're taking a deliberate timeout to quiet your mind, whether through focusing on your breath, repeating a mantra or affirmation, or simply watching your thoughts float by like clouds.

The benefits? They're absolutely remarkable. My research and clinical experience have shown that regular meditation promotes the following:

- Lowers blood pressure as effectively as some medications
- Reduces anxiety and depression symptoms up to 40%
- Improves sleep quality dramatically

- Boosts immune system function
- Evens your emotional spectrum
- Increases your ability to handle stress with grace

The Wonders of Mindfulness

Now, mindfulness is something entirely different – though equally powerful. Think of mindfulness as bringing your full attention to whatever you're doing right now. Whether you're washing dishes, walking the dog, or sitting in traffic, mindfulness means being fully present in that moment.

What I love about mindfulness is that you can practice it anywhere, anytime. No special cushion or quiet room required! When you're mindful, you're:

- Fully experiencing life rather than running on autopilot
- Living in the present moment, not the past (anger) or the future (worry)
- Catching stress perceptions/reactions before they spiral (from molehills to mountains)
- Building stronger connections with others through better listening
- Making better decisions because you're more aware Finding joy in simple moments you might have missed before
- Seeing wonder and awe (even curiosity) in the present moment

Why You Need Both Types of Meditation in Your Resiliency Toolkit

Here's the beautiful thing: meditation and mindfulness complement each other perfectly. Meditation is like going to the gym for your mind—it builds your mental muscles in a focused

43

way. Mindfulness is like taking those stronger muscles out into the world and using them throughout your day.

In my stress management and resiliency workshops, I often see people gravitate toward one practice or the other at first. That's perfectly fine! Start where you're comfortable. If sitting still for meditation feels challenging, begin with mindfulness exercises during your daily activities. If you love the structure of meditation, start there and gradually bring mindfulness into your day.

Remember, there's no "right" way to do either practice. The key is consistency and kindness toward yourself as you explore these tools. Your mind will wander during meditation—that's normal! You'll forget to be mindful sometimes—that's human! What matters is gently returning to the practice, one breath, one moment at a time.

Both meditation and mindfulness are gifts you give yourself in a world that often forgets to slow down. They're not about emptying your mind or achieving some perfect state of zen. They're about living more fully, loving more deeply, and finding peace in the midst of whatever life brings your way.

Start small, be patient, and watch the magic unfold. Your mind—and your stress levels—will thank you.

5

Getting Started with Meditation: Strategies for Success

Here's something crucial I want you to understand: meditation is not a one-size-fits-all prescription! It's more like a vast garden with many different paths, each leading to its own unique sanctuary of peace. Let me break this down into what I consider two fundamental approaches to meditation.

Exclusive Meditation: The Power of Single-Pointed Focus

Think of exclusive meditation as a spotlight in a dark room. When you shine that spotlight on one specific object, everything else naturally fades into the background. This might be your breath (my personal favorite), a meaningful mantra, or even the mesmerizing flame of a candle. I've had students who find their meditation in the rhythmic motion of running or swimming – what I call "meditation in motion." Exclusive meditation means to exclude all thoughts from your mind but one (e.g., your breathing, or a mantra/affirmation).

You see, the beauty of exclusive meditation lies in its simplicity. By giving your mind one clear focal point, you're essentially saying to all those racing thoughts, "Thank you, but not right now." It's particularly effective for my clients and students who describe their minds as "constantly buzzing," or those just beginning their meditation journey. If you are looking for a simple mantra or affirmation phrase, consider this one:

"My body is calm and relaxed." Repeat this phrase to yourself each time you exhale.

Inclusive Meditation: The Art of Mindful Awareness

Now, inclusive meditation—this is when we open the curtains and let in all the light. Rather than narrowing our focus to a single thought, we expand it. This approach, which includes mindfulness meditation, is like becoming the sky that simply watches the clouds (your thoughts and feelings) drift by. The key to mindfulness is to observe without judgment.

Some people describe mindfulness as if they are watching a slow-moving river, a metaphorical river of thoughts. But rather watching the river, mindfulness invites you to step back and watch yourself watch the river of thoughts, without judgment or emotional attachment. In my stress management programs, I've observed how this practice helps people develop what I call "emotional intelligence through awareness." You're not trying to change or judge your experiences; you're simply acknowledging them with the compassionate curiosity of an observer. It's a powerful tool for developing self-understanding and emotional resilience. Observing without judgment can be challenging because the ego loves to judge, hence the expression, domesticate your ego.

Let me share something I've learned over my years of practice and teaching: there's no need to choose between these approaches. In fact, I encourage you to think of them as different instruments in your personal orchestra of well-being, or different tools in your resiliency toolbox. Some days, you might need the focused clarity of exclusive meditation; other times, the expansive awareness of inclusive practice might better serve your needs.

Remember, the goal isn't to perfect a technique—it's to find your path to inner peace and enhanced well-being. As I always say in my workshops, "The best meditation practice is the one you'll actually do."

Did Someone Say Insight Meditation?

By some accounts there is a third type of meditation, called insight meditation. Many people, including me, consider it to be a by-product of exclusive and inclusive meditation. Here is what happens: when you can really calm the mind, specifically the ego—the gatekeeper or censor of the conscious mind—new insights or intuitive thoughts may surface from the unconscious mind (or beyond) that give clarity to your personal view of existence. Some people call this acquired wisdom or "insights;" others call it "enlightenment." As you can imagine, it takes a lot of practice to calm the waters of the mind to the point of clear reflection that offers deep insights. Remember, you cannot demand enlightenment, but you can prepare for it. Hence the wonderful Chinese proverb, "When the student is ready, the teacher will come." In the meantime, focusing on your breath, repeating a calm mantra, or being mindful of the present moment is the primary goal. Anything else is icing on the cake.

Is Guided Mental Imagery
a Form of Meditation?

Well, yes and no. Guided mental imagery is considered its own type of relaxation technique, based on following suggested verbal guidance (e.g., audio files, podcasts, etc.). The purpose is to engage all of your senses (e.g., sight, sound smell, touch) by imagining various experiences through your mind's eye. Examples might include walking along an ocean beach, sitting by a calm body of water, or walking through a cathedral forest. Conversely, and historically, meditation has been primarily self-guided. In the past decade, as various stress management techniques became increasingly popular in the American culture, including meditation, many therapists, stress management teachers, wellness professionals and even celebrities have created guided meditations, including a host of breathing exercises, to promote relaxation. Please keep in mind that not all guided mental imagery exercises are considered guided meditations, and not all guided meditations are considered mental imagery exercises.

In the larger sense, when you are engaged, focused and in the flow of a guided mental imagery session you are, in essence, meditating. Some people, particularly when starting a meditation practice, prefer the assistance of verbal suggestions, such as diaphragmatic breathing instructions, to help stay focused. Bottom line: Find a method(s) and style that best works for you.

A Meditation Story Worth Sharing

After the school shooting in Columbine High School occurred, I was invited to speak at several high schools and middle schools to teach a host of stress management and relaxation skills. Meditation was one such skill that I shared with students and teachers alike. In one school program, called HealthQuest, that spanned the entire school year, I was a co-facilitator. I will never forget the time one student came up to me at the end of the course and said, "Dr. Seaward, I finally get meditation." I replied, "You do? Please share." He went on to say, "I get it, I get meditation. It's like deleting old text messages and emails."

Boredom Is Part of the Meditation Process

Everyone (no exception) gets bored starting or continuing their meditation practice. Everyone! The reason is that the ego-based mind loves and seeks stimulation. It thrives on stimulation. Meditation resets the mind by lowering the threshold for calm and inner peace. This reset requires minimal sensory stimulation and non-judgment (two things the ego-mind craves, if not demands), hence the boredom. This resetting process drives the ego-based mind nuts. At this stage you may find yourself wanting to quit, thinking meditation doesn't work. Be patient. Boredom is not only part of the process, it is an essential part. But it is only a temporary stage. With practice you will get beyond it and enjoy the fruits of your re-focused labor.

Strategies for Success

One of the most common challenges I hear from my students isn't about the meditation techniques themselves, but rather about establishing and maintaining a consistent practice. In this chapter, I'll share proven strategies that have helped thousands of my clients transform meditation from an occasional activity into a nourishing daily practice.

The First "Rule" of Meditation: Just Show Up

Consistency is key when cultivating a meditation practice. Make it a habit to set aside time regularly to sit down and meditate, regardless of how much time you have available. The important thing is to establish a regular routine.

Start by setting a time limit that works for your schedule but remain flexible. Start small (as in baby steps). Start with five minutes of simply observing your breathing. If five minutes seems like an eternity (and it may), try two minutes and slowly add a minute each day for a couple of weeks. Everyone can sit for a minute or two and observe their breathing.

Many people find that thirty minutes per session is ideal, but don't stress if your schedule only allows for fifteen minutes on certain days. The key is to go with the flow and avoid getting caught up in the exact duration.

The most important thing is to simply "show up" and be present for your practice, even if it's for a shorter period. Over time, as meditation becomes a regular part of your day, you may find that you naturally want to expand the duration of your sessions. But don't worry about that in the beginning—focus on making meditation a consistent habit first.

Remember, the goal is not to achieve perfection, but to develop a sustainable practice that you can stick to over the long term. Be gentle with yourself, celebrate small victories, and enjoy the process of cultivating greater mindfulness and inner peace.

The Three R's of Mindfulness

When your mind wanders (which it will), remember the three R's:

1. **Recognize** when your focus has drifted,

2. **Release** any expectations, and

3. **Return** your attention to your breathing.

This gentle, self-compassionate approach can transform meditation from a frustrating task into a rewarding journey. This also becomes a great mantra: "Recognize, Release, Return." If it helps, type these words up on a piece of paper and place them by you when you meditate.

Create Your Meditation Space

Your environment plays a crucial role in supporting your meditation practice. While you can meditate anywhere, having a dedicated space signals to your brain that it's time to shift into a more contemplative state. The resiliency term for this is "healthy boundaries!"

- Choose a quiet area or corner of the room where you won't be disturbed.
- Keep the space clutter-free and visually calming (even if your eyes are closed).
- Consider natural light or soft lighting.
- Try playing soft instrumental music as white noise.
- Maintain a comfortable room temperature.
- Have necessary props readily available (cushion, timer, blanket).
- Keep a pad of paper and pen handy to write down things that come to mind while you sit. You may find

that a wandering mind will create the most amazing To Do list.

- Most importantly, minimize all distractions and leave your screen devices and cell phone in another room. You will survive without these for a short period of time. Again, think "healthy boundaries."

You don't need an entire room—even a small corner of your bedroom can serve as your sanctuary. The key is consistency in using this space primarily for meditation.

Find Your Optimal Time

Timing is also important. Many people find that starting their day with meditation sets a positive tone and helps them approach challenges with a calm, focused mindset throughout the rest of the day. However, it's best to avoid meditating after a large meal or when you're physically or emotionally drained. Ultimately, the best time to meditate is when you can consistently show up for your practice. However, certain times typically work better:

- Early morning, before the day's demands begin
- Lunch break, as a midday reset
- Evening, to decompress from the day
- Transition periods (arriving home from work, before starting dinner)
- Start Small and Growing
- Begin with just 5 minutes daily
- Increase duration by 1-2 minutes each week
- Build up to 15-20 minutes as your baseline
- Consider two shorter sessions instead of one longer session

Building Momentum

Track Progress

- Keep a simple meditation log (even notes on your calendar)
- Note duration, time of day, and type of practice
- Record brief observations about your experience
- Review monthly to identify patterns and progress

Create Accountability

- Join a meditation group or class
- Use a meditation app (e.g., Mindspace, Insight-Timer, etc.) with reminders
- Share your commitment with close family members or friends
- Find a meditation buddy for check-ins

Deepen Your Practice

- Attend occasional workshops or retreats
- Read inspiring books about meditation (see Appendix A for some suggestions)
- Connect with experienced practitioners
- Journal about your insights and challenges

FUN FACTS ABOUT THE MEDITATION

- Meditation is now shown to slow down the aging process by increasing the integrity of the DNA's telomeres.
- Meditation helps improve memory.
- Meditation is a proven tool to reduce chronic pain.
- Meditation enhances the integrity of your immune system.
- Meditation reduces hypertension (high blood pressure).
- Meditation helps decision making and creativity.
- Meditation is one of the most popular mind-body techniques for optimal wellness.
- As of 2024 well over 38 million people meditate regularly in the US.
- World Meditation Day is May 21.

Find What Works for You

The key to a successful meditation practice is to find what works best for you. Meditation is a deeply personal practice, so be patient, stay open-minded, and trust the process. With regular practice, you'll begin to experience the profound benefits of mindfulness and self-awareness.

On a personal note: Decades ago, when I first tried a sitting meditation practice, I played some relaxing acoustic music as a type of white noise. What began as a five-minute practice soon turned into ten minutes, then days later, fifteen minutes, and before I knew it, I was sitting comfortably for a half hour. It also really helped to have a pen and paper by my side to write down ideas, thoughts, and items for my To Do list. Once they were on paper, I could forget about them and return my attention to my breath. Now, sometimes for variety I listen to guided meditations (even my own). Once a week I do the rainbow meditation, based on the colors of the chakras (or the body's energy centers). I find it's nice to have some options. Interestingly, I also found that on the occasional day where I had to skip the morning meditation due to some pressing obligation, I began to get a headache in the afternoon. That was an important sign of just how important my meditation practice was. It has been my happy place ever since.

6

Dealing with Common Meditation Challenges

Meditation is a powerful practice, but like any worthwhile endeavor, embarking on a meditation journey isn't without its hurdles. For those new to meditation, the path can sometimes feel daunting. The contrast between the calm, centered state that meditation promises, and the initial experiences of restlessness, distraction, or frustration can be stark. It's important to remember that your mind is used to constant stimulation, so when you ask it to be quiet, it rebels a bit. This resistance is natural and a part of the process.

It's crucial to approach meditation and mindfulness practices with patience, understanding, and a healthy dose of self-compassion. Recognizing and preparing for potential obstacles can significantly smooth your path and help you cultivate a sustainable, rewarding practice. By understanding these obstacles and learning strategies to overcome them, you'll be better equipped to navigate the early stages of your practice and reap the profound benefits that regular meditation can offer.

Managing Expectations

In our fast-paced culture, with immediate gratification as the norm, people often expect dramatic, overnight transformation from meditation, but the reality is quite different. It's like the old joke about the person who wants patience; "I want patience and I want it right now!" Meditation simply doesn't work that way.

Meditation is a skill, much like playing a musical instrument or mastering a sport. The first time you try, it's nowhere near as graceful or effortless as when you've been practicing for weeks, months, or years. One of the key challenges is to let go of expectations about the meditation process. There are no instant results; progress takes time and consistency.

Patience, discipline, and dedication are essential for experiencing the true benefits of meditation. It's easy to fall into the trap of wanting the rewards without putting in the work. But genuine effort and commitment are crucial. I'll level with you—meditation can be difficult. It takes regular practice to become proficient, just like any other skill. It requires dedication, perseverance, and a willingness to face occasional discomfort head-on. But as most anyone who stays with it will tell you, it is well worth it.

Restlessness and Discomfort

Many people resist meditation, claiming they don't have the time or can't sit still. However, these are the exact reasons why meditation is so beneficial. If you feel restless or struggle to focus, know that you're in good company—even experienced meditators face these challenges.

The first step is to find a comfortable position. Comfort is paramount in meditation; if you're not at ease, experiment until you find a posture that allows you to relax. Sitting on a cushion or pillow with your back up against a wall is most common, but some people prefer to lay down (like *shavasana*, or "corpse pose" in Hatha Yoga).

Falling Asleep While Meditating?

If you happen to feel drowsy or even fall asleep while meditating, no worries; you're in good company. This happens to practically everyone at some point in the practice of meditation. When I taught relaxation techniques to college students and Olympic athletes, I can't tell you how many times they fell asleep—I knew because they were snoring! Mindfulness expert Jon Kabat-Zinn calls falling asleep while meditation an "occupational hazard." No worries. It happens! And if it happens to you, it's not a sign of failure. Most likely it's a sign that you are mentally exhausted. If this should happen, simply get up and walk around a bit, get some fresh air, drink some water (dehydration leads to mental fatigue) and then come back to the meditation experience more refreshed. Perhaps try meditating with your eyes open, with a gentle gaze on an object like a candle flame or circular-shaped object like a colorful mandala. If, however, you find yourself falling asleep frequently, it's very likely you are not getting enough sleep during normal sleeping hours. If this is the case, consider practicing some good "sleep hygiene" habits, including a media curfew an hour before bedtime, regular sleep hours, quality bedding (down comforter, down pillow and high thread count sheets), and a cool, dark sleep environment.

Remember, it's okay if you fall asleep occasionally; it simply means your body needs rest. Honor this. Here are a few more meditation suggestions to consider:

- Meditate at a time of day when you're naturally alert.
- Try a standing or walking meditation.
- Maintain a sitting posture with your spine upright/ straight.
- Consider listening to a guided meditation.
- Consider listening to nature sounds (e.g., ocean waves, rainforest rain).

"Am I Doing This Right?"

A common question is, "Am I doing this right?" The simple answer is: Yes! Meditation is about being present and aware, focusing on your breathing. There's no one-size-fits-all approach, so don't get bogged down by dogma or trying to follow a specific system. Experiment until you find a technique and style that resonate with you.

Boredom and Restlessness

As stated earlier (but it bears repeating), the first and perhaps most prevalent challenge is boredom. Our culture doesn't encourage sitting quietly; instead, it pushes us to constantly engage our five senses through technology and external stimuli. So, when you try to unplug and focus internally, boredom is almost guaranteed.

- Begin with one minute and gradually work your way up to five or ten minutes.
- Start with movement-based practices (e.g., walking, swimming, etc.).
- Gradually transition to stillness (e.g., sitting quietly with your back to the wall).
- Use shorter sessions (e.g., five minutes) more frequently.
- Stretch your hamstring and lower back muscles to reset your mind.
- Practice self-compassion when restlessness arises.

"I Can't Stop Thinking"

Internal distractions often manifest as unceasing thoughts. To manage these distractions, it's really helpful to keep a notepad and pen nearby during your meditation. When urgent thoughts arise (and most likely they will), you can quickly jot them down if you need to and return to your breathing. Once down on paper, you can let those thoughts go and know you can refer to the list later after you get done meditating.

Remember, the goal isn't to eliminate thoughts, but to change your relationship with them. Through regular practice, you'll develop the ability to observe your thoughts and emotions without judgment and without becoming entangled in them, ultimately reducing your stress response. You can also:

- Understand that the goal isn't to stop or control your thoughts.
- Use thoughts as opportunities to practice returning to your breath.
- Consider guided meditations initially.
- Remember that even experienced meditators have busy minds.

How to Deal with Strong Emotions While Meditating

On occasion, when meditating, you may be faced with one or more uncomfortable emotions, such as anger, doubt, fear, sadness, or even grief. This is normal! The first reaction to these emotional encounters is sometimes to stop your meditation session or quit meditation altogether. Experts strongly suggest otherwise. Respond, don't react. If and when this happens, take a few slow deep breaths and become the observer. Remember, you are not your thoughts or your emotions. First observe, then try to identify the specific emotion you are feeling. Then label it. If there is more than one emotion, label it with the word "mix." If you cannot put your finger on exactly what the feeling is, label it as "Blah." Experts say that when you can observe emotions, you become better at processing them without judgement and then moving through (releasing) them. The bottom line is this: Keep meditating.

External Distractions

External distractions are things like a barking dog, a ringing phone, incoming text alerts, or even family members or housemates who interrupt your private space. While it may seem impossible to eliminate all external distractions, it is possible to minimize them, as part of your healthy boundaries practice. When necessary, remind those whom you live with to honor your meditation time. Establish a sacred, tech-free meditation space, but also learn to acknowledge and release these external stimuli when they occur. Control what you can, let go of the rest. This practice of acknowledging and letting go of distractions can actually strengthen your meditation skills over time, teaching you to remain centered and calm amidst life's inevitable disturbances.

Create A Neutral Soundscape

Removing all distractions from the meditation experience is ideal, but sometimes this is not entirely possible, particularly in a noisy environment. To balance out sonic distractions some people use white noise. White noise is a sound that contains all the sound frequencies in the audible spectrum, used to neutralize existing sounds—in essence to cancel them out by blending them all together. This may sound complicated but it really isn't. For example, you may find it helpful while meditating to play a recording of ocean waves or a babbling brook to cancel out the sounds of your neighbor's lawn mower. If the ambient sounds in your meditation environment are less than ideal, please consider some natural sound recordings to neutralize your soundscape and enhance your meditation experience. Some white noise audio files now include the 432 hertz frequency, which offers a more harmonious and soothing experience.

Reclaiming the Lost Art of Stillness

The mind craves stimulation. This can be seen with our daily fascination with consuming untold hours of content on the Internet and streaming devices. Sensory stimulation can be wonderful. Too much, however, can be exhausting and nerve-wracking. Just as the mind craves stimulation, the mind also craves stillness. Not only does it crave stillness, it requires it! The mind requires downtime for information processing, long term memory storage, mental clarity and the proverbial sense of "peace of mind."

Sensory bombardment in today's culture may seem like a novelty, but it's nothing new. For eons, sages and wisdom keepers have reminded us of the need for calm and serenity. References to the importance of stillness, specifically, a still mind, can be found in nearly every ancient text. To reclaim this lost art, we first need to recognize and honor its essential importance for our mental health. Then we need to designate a time each day to sit still, pause and catch our breath, before the onslaught of sensory stimulation begins once again. In the words of the mystic Rumi, "When I am silent, I fall into the place where everything is music."

Signs of Progress

The benefits of meditation may not be immediate (remember, skills take practice) but results do happen rather quickly. While it's important not to become attached to specific outcomes or benefits, within six to eight weeks of regular practice, you may notice some or all of the following:

- Increased awareness of thought patterns
- More space between triggers and reactions to various triggers
- Better sleep quality
- Enhanced stress resilience
- Improved emotional regulation
  Greater sense of overall well-being (10%+ happier)

Remember that progress in meditation isn't linear. Some days will feel easier than others (e.g. weekends), and that's perfectly normal. The key is to maintain consistency in your practice while holding your experience with gentle awareness and acceptance. By implementing these practical strategies and approaching your practice with patience and persistence, you'll develop a sustainable meditation habit that serves as a reliable foundation for managing life's inevitable stresses and challenges.

7

Beyond Anxiety: Mindfulness and Meditation as a Path to Self-Discovery

The Bridge Between Practice and Daily Life

Meditation is a powerful catalyst for self-discovery and personal growth, but its true value emerges when we seamlessly integrate it into our daily lives. Allow me to share an illuminating experience that underscores this crucial point.

During my time teaching Olympic athletes mindfulness and mental training, we began in a serene, controlled environment. This quiet space provided an ideal setting for them to learn and hone their skills without external distractions. However, the competitive arena presents an entirely different challenge—a cacophony of sounds, a sea of faces, the presence of stiff competition, and a myriad of potential distractions.

This stark contrast serves as a perfect metaphor for our meditation journey. While we often cultivate our practice in tranquil settings, the real challenge—and indeed, the most profound benefit—lies in transferring these skills into the vibrant tapestry of our daily lives.

62

The Ultimate Goal: Presence in Every Moment

The essence of meditation extends far beyond finding peace in a controlled environment. Its true aim is to foster a state of presence that permeates every facet of our existence. This means being fully engaged whether we're:

- immersed in conversation,
- navigating rush hour traffic,
- absorbing the pages of a captivating book,
- watching a movie (without googling the cast's previous accomplishments),
- or even performing seemingly mundane tasks like washing dishes, doing laundry, or vacuuming the house.

Consider how often people's minds wander during conversations, or how distracted drivers can become on busy roads. These everyday scenarios exemplify the transformative potential of mindfulness in action. Being fully present in the now moment is a gift that keeps on giving.

Cultivating Mindful Habits

Creating mindful habits (conscious choices) is about bridging the gap between our sacred meditation space and the world we inhabit. It's about maintaining a present-moment focus during any activity, rather than allowing our minds to drift aimlessly between past regrets and future anxieties. When we're truly present, we become:

- more effective in our actions,
- more authentic to our human spirit,

- more engaged in our personal relationships,
- more deeply connected to others and our environment,
- and often, more content with our current circumstances.

This transfer of skills from meditation to daily life is where genuine transformation takes root. It's not always a smooth journey—our modern world teems with distractions and demands on our attention. Moreover, relentless marketing ploys often fuel our personal insecurities, giving the ego plenty of content to become distracted and obsessed with.

The good news, however, is that with dedicated practice we can learn to navigate our days with heightened awareness and intention, infusing the calm clarity of meditation into every moment.

The ultimate goal of meditation and mindfulness isn't just to find peace in a controlled environment, but to build resilience and cultivate presence in every aspect of our lives.

Helpful Strategies for Mindful Living

Set Daily Intentions

Start each day with a simple yet powerful phrase like, "Today, I intend to be present." This gentle reminder helps anchor your awareness to the here and now, fostering a deeper connection to your experiences.

Practice Mindful Reflection

Take time each evening to reflect on your day. Not to judge, but to observe how you can refine your behaviors for tomorrow's practice. This reflection can include identifying three things you are grateful for. Research shows that focusing on gratitude helps to rewire the brain for peace and relaxation.

This reflection allows you to:

- recognize patterns in your thoughts and actions
- make conscious adjustments to your routine
- cultivate a more mindful and intentional way of living
- become more appreciative of positive things in your life

Create Mindfulness Triggers

Associate everyday activities like brewing coffee or tea, or waiting at traffic lights, with brief moments of mindfulness. Use these as opportunities to check in with yourself and realign with your intention to be present.

Practice Micro-Meditations

Incorporate short, one-to-two-minute meditation breaks into your day. These can be as simple as taking a few conscious breaths, doing a quick body scan, or even a gratitude reflection.

Engage Your Senses

Regularly pause to fully experience your environment through all five senses. This simple act can quickly ground you in the present moment.

By consistently setting intentions, reflecting on our progress, and implementing these practical strategies, we create a continuous loop of growth and self-awareness. This ongoing practice allows us to gradually extend the peace and clarity of our formal meditation into every corner of our lives, transforming not just our inner world, but our entire lived experience.

PART THREE

Mindfulness and Meditation Techniques for Anxiety and Stress Management

"Meditation helps me to calm down."

– Lady Gaga

"The greatest weapon against stress is our ability to choose one thought over another."

– William James

8

Mindfulness Techniques

Every transformation begins with a single step. Let me share the story of Mark, an accomplished artist who helped design several of my book and audio covers. Like many of us, Mark initially viewed meditation with skepticism, dismissing it as just another wellness trend. Despite his creative talents, he struggled with chronic pain and stress that threatened to overshadow his work and his joy in life.

What makes Mark's story compelling isn't just his eventual embrace of mindfulness and meditation, but the authentic journey that led him there. It wasn't until physical pain pushed him to his limits that he truly opened himself to change. This is a pattern I've observed repeatedly: sometimes we need to hit rock bottom before we're ready to explore new paths. Today, Mark does his meditation practice daily for at least thirty minutes, and he has become one of meditation's best advocates.

The Foundations of Mindfulness

Mindfulness isn't just a practice—it's a gateway to experiencing life more fully. At its core lie three fundamental techniques that anyone can master.

Breath Awareness: Your Natural Anchor

Your breath is always with you, making it the perfect focal point for meditation. Rather than try to control your breathing, simply observe its natural rhythm. Notice how your breath moves through your body, the subtle expansion of your lungs, the gentle rise and fall of your abdomen. This awareness alone can create a profound shift in your mental state.

Here's something interesting about breathing: most Americans are "chest breathers," using primarily their upper lungs. While this might look impressive, it actually triggers a subtle stress response in your body. Instead, focus on diaphragmatic breathing—or what I call "belly breathing."

When you breathe diaphragmatically, your stomach gently expands like a balloon with each inhalation. This natural breathing pattern activates your vagus nerve, the master switch of your relaxation response. It's how we breathe when we're sleeping, and how young children breathe before self-consciousness about one's body appearance sets in.

Body Scanning: A Journey Within

Imagine having a flashlight of awareness that you can shine on any part of your body. This is body scanning—a systematic exploration of physical sensations that deepens your connection with yourself. Start at your toes and slowly work upward, or begin at your head and travel down. Pay attention to areas of tension, temperature, or tingling. You might be surprised by what you discover.

Sensory Awareness: Awakening to Life

Our senses offer five different doorways into the present moment. Take a moment now to notice the play of light and shadow in your environment, the ambient sounds reaching your ears, the texture of your clothing against your skin. This heightened awareness transforms ordinary moments into opportunities for mindfulness.

Mindful Walking: Moving Meditation

Transform your daily walk into a meditation by bringing full awareness to each step. Feel the ground beneath your feet, notice the rhythm of your movement, observe the world around you with fresh eyes. This practice grounds you in the present moment while connecting you with your environment.

Mindful Conversation: The Art of Presence

Most people listen to respond, rather than understand. Practice mindful conversations by giving others your full attention. Notice not just their words, but their tone, body language, and the emotions behind their message. This deep listening creates space for empathy and genuine connection.

Visualization: Your Mind's Sanctuary

Create a mental haven you can visit anytime. Picture a peaceful scene in vivid detail—perhaps a sunlit beach or a quiet forest. Engage all your senses: hear the waves or rustling leaves, feel the warmth or cool breeze, smell the salt air or pine needles. This practice offers a powerful refuge during stressful moments.

The Ripple Effect

As Mark discovered, the benefits of mindfulness extend far beyond the meditation cushion. Within a few weeks of starting his meditation practice, the chronic pain in his lower back subsided, replaced by a genuine lightness of being. Now when I see him, he proudly shares the benefits of his daily practice, his calm face and broad smile reflecting the inner peace he's found.

This transformation illustrates a fundamental truth: mindfulness isn't about escaping life's challenges—it's about developing the resilience to meet them with grace. Through regular practice, you build an inner sanctuary that remains stable even when life feels chaotic. To repeat the words of the mystic Rumi, "In the chaos, build a temple of love."

Remember, mindfulness is a journey, not a destination. Start where you are, with what you have, in this moment. Like Mark, you might find that the simple act of paying attention can transform your entire world, making it a happy, more comfortable place to inhabit.

9

Essential Meditation Techniques

In my forty-five years of teaching stress management and resiliency training, I've found that there is no one style or technique of meditation for everyone. Just as each person experiences stress differently, so too does each individual connect with meditation techniques in his or her own way. The following time-tested methods offer various pathways to inner peace and stress reduction. I encourage you to explore these techniques with an open mind, finding the approaches that resonate most deeply with you.

Breath Awareness Meditation

The foundation of all meditation practices is the breath. This technique's beauty lies in its simplicity and accessibility—it can be practiced anywhere, at any time.

Start by finding a comfortable seated position, either in a chair with your feet flat on the floor or cross-legged on a cushion. Allow your spine to rise naturally, as if an invisible thread were gently pulling the crown of your head toward the ceiling. Rest your hands comfortably in your lap.

Close your eyes or maintain a soft gaze downward. Begin by simply observing your natural breathing pattern without attempting to change it. Notice the sensation of air moving through your nostrils, the gentle rise and fall of your chest and abdomen. When your mind wanders—and it will—gently guide your attention back to your breath without judgment.

Practice this for five to ten minutes initially, gradually extending the duration as you become more comfortable with the technique.

Body Scan Meditation

This powerful method helps release physical tension while cultivating deep awareness of the mind-body connection. It's particularly effective for those who hold stress in their bodies or struggle with sleep.

Lie down in a comfortable position, arms at your sides, palms facing up. Beginning at your toes, systematically direct your attention to each part of your body, consciously releasing tension as you go. Notice any sensations present—tingling, warmth, pressure, or perhaps numbness. Don't try to change these sensations; simply observe them with curious attention.

Move slowly through your feet, ankles, calves, knees, thighs, and so on, until you reach the crown of your head. If you notice an area of particular tension, breathe into that space, imagining the breath dissolving the tightness with each exhale.

Loving-Kindness Meditation (Metta)

In our high-pressure world, this heart-centered practice serves as a powerful antidote to stress-induced negativity and self-criticism. It cultivates compassion for ourselves and others, promoting emotional resilience.

Begin in a comfortable seated position. Start by directing loving-kindness toward yourself, silently repeating thoughts such as:

- *May I be happy.*
- *May I be healthy.*
- *May I be safe.*
- *May I be at peace.*

Allow these words to resonate in your heart. After a few minutes, expand these wishes to someone you love, then to a neutral person, to someone challenging, and finally to all beings everywhere. (For a longer version of the loving-kindness meditation, please see Appendix D.)

Walking Meditation

For those who find sitting meditation challenging, walking meditation offers an active alternative that can be equally profound. This practice is particularly beneficial for those who spend long hours at desks or experience anxiety when sitting still.

Choose a quiet path or space where you can walk slowly without interruption. As you walk, bring your attention to the sensations in your feet and legs. Notice the shifting of weight, the lifting and placing of each foot, the rhythm of your movement. When your mind wanders, return your focus to these physical sensations.

Practical Implementation Tips

- Start small: Begin with 5-10 minutes daily rather than attempting lengthy sessions immediately.
- Create consistency: Choose a specific time each day for your practice.
- Be patient: Like any skill, meditation becomes easier with regular practice.
- Stay curious: Notice which techniques resonate with you and why.
- Maintain gentle discipline: When resistance arises, acknowledge it without letting it derail your practice.

When Life Gets in the Way

Life inevitably throws curveballs that can disrupt our routines. Here are strategies for maintaining your practice during challenging times:

When Time Is Limited

- Do one-minute meditation breaks.

- Practice mindfulness (present centeredness) during daily activities.
- Use simplified techniques (three conscious breaths).
- Remember that something is better than nothing.

During High-Stress Periods

- Seek support from a mental health professional if needed.
- Increase frequency rather than duration.
- Use the guided meditations in this program for extra support.
- Focus on grounding techniques.
- Practice Self-Compassion: Be extra gentle with yourself.

PART FOUR

Cultivating Calm: Practices for Lasting Peace

"In meditation, I can let go of everything. I'm just dipping into that powerful source that creates everything. I take a little bath in it."

– Hugh Jackman (actor)

10

Practical Mindfulness and Meditation Exercises

The following are simple and quick mindfulness exercises that may help calm your nerves and promote a sense of inner peace. For simplicity's sake, they are divided into five categories. While these exercises are designed to be accessible, remember that mindfulness is a skill that develops with consistent practice.

Each exercise is intentionally brief and can be completed in a short amount of time and even while participating in daily activities. The categories are structured to address different aspects of stress and anxiety, offering varied approaches to cultivating mental calm and emotional balance. Some exercises focus on breath awareness, others on the body, and some on present-moment perception.

As you work through these exercises, approach them with an attitude of gentle curiosity — there's no "perfect" way or ideal protocol for practicing mindfulness. Remember, it's normal for your mind to wander. The key is to return to the present moment whenever you notice your thoughts drifting. Simply acknowledge this without judgment and gently guide your attention back to the exercise.

The goal with each of these examples is to develop a more balanced and compassionate relationship with your inner experiences. With regular practice, these techniques can help recalibrate your thinking processes to help you build resilience, improve emotional regulation, and create moments of peace in your daily life.

Mindful Breathing

Conscious breathing is one of the best ways to calm the nervous system. An old Chinese proverb reminds us that "There are over 40 different ways to breathe," and nearly all have to do with promoting relaxation. Here are a few styles to try as additional tools in your resiliency toolkit:

4 x 4 (Box Breathing)

This exercise invites you to focus on the four phases of each breath (inhalation, pause, exhalation, pause) with a count of four seconds for each phase: four seconds for the in-breath, four seconds pause (hold), four seconds for the out-breath, followed by a four second count as you hold your breath before you inhale once again. Repeat this cycle four times.

Belly Breathing

As a rule, Americans don't breathe with the focus of the breath on the stomach area (also known as "diaphragmatic breathing"). Rather, Americans tend to be thoracic breathers, with the focus on the upper chest. Whether you are a man or a woman, American cultural and social norms favor a big chest and a small stomach. Thoracic breathing tends to promote a faster heart rate and higher blood pressure (physiological stress) due to increased pressure on the sternum (chest bone) and nerve bundles underneath or behind it. Belly breathing shifts the focus of your breath below the heart to the stomach area. Physiologically, this is the preferred style of breathing. While it may feel a bit odd extending your stomach as you breathe, remember, this is how you breathe when you are asleep.

Shamanic Breathing

Deep in the Peruvian Andes, shamans have been teaching a breathing style for relaxation for ages. It goes something like this: Each exhalation should be twice as long as your inhalation. Breathe in for a count of four seconds, and then slowly exhale for a count of eight seconds. Repeat this for four cycles. If you wish you can increase the number of seconds for the in-breath, (e.g., five or six seconds) and then double that as you exhale (e.g., ten to twelve seconds).

Sixty Second Breath Count

This exercise invites you to count the number of breath cycles you take for a full minute. Typically, the average number ranges between twelve and fourteen cycles. Higher levels of stress will promote a higher number of breath cycles per minute (e.g., twenty to thirty short, shallow breaths). Conversely, when one is very relaxed, this number may decrease to four to six breath cycles per second.

Note: Recently health experts have noticed that many Americans have become "breath holders," either holding their breath after they inhale or holding their breath after they exhale. Most of these people don't even realize they are doing this. This style of breathing is also known as "anxiety breathing," and its anything but relaxing.

Infinity Symbol Breathing

This style of mindfulness breathing begins with a mental image of the infinity shape (a large figure 8 on its side). You begin by looking at the midpoint of the far left side of the symbol, inhaling as you follow the shape up and then down toward the center. At the center, you exhale, following the direction of the shape to the middle of the far right side. Then inhale as you follow the shape up and back to the center, exhaling at the center, then down to where you began on the left side. Repeat several times, each time with a very slow, deep breath.

Body Awareness

One of the best mindfulness techniques involves fully engaging one or more of your five senses to enter into the present moment. Perhaps the most popular is the mindfulness body scan, as mentioned earlier.

Body Scan

From head to toes, slowly conduct a sensory inventory of the muscle tension/muscle relaxation in all your body regions. Start with the head, move down to the neck and shoulders, then focus on the chest and stomach areas, followed by your arms and hands, then your lower torso, upper legs, and lower legs, and conclude with your feet. Does your body feel any more relaxed after this scan than before you started?

5 Senses Check-in

This mindfulness exercise invites you to go through each of your five senses and deepen the awareness of your surroundings through sight, sound, taste, touch and smell. Some people call this the 5+4+3+2+1 mindfulness game. Start by identifying 5 things you can see, then 4 things you can feel, then 3 things you can hear, then 2 things you can smell, and finally, 1 thing you can taste.

You can augment this exercise by including these additional activities:

- Take a moment to listen to the ambient sounds around you, music, birds, etc.
- Walk into the kitchen, pick up something to eat/drink and really taste the food or beverage you place in your mouth before swallowing it.
- Get up from your chair and consciously walk up or down the nearest flight of stairs, feeling what muscles in your legs are being used to move from place to place.
- Keep a polished tumbled stone in your pocket or desktop and pick it up and rub the smooth surface over your fingertips for several moments.
- Place a collection of new favorite, colorful landscape photos on your computer desktop as screensavers and savor their colors.
- Place a vial of your favorite aromatherapy fragrance nearby and smell the scent as you breath in to relaxation.

Guided Meditations and Visualizations

It's always nice to close your eyes and take a quick break away from a stressful moment. That's where guided mental imagery and scripted meditations come in. Some people call these a mental vacation. Others refer to it as a relaxation Rx. We will provide some of my favorite guided visualizations in the audio version of this book. In Chapter 11, I include QR codes that you can scan with your phone to play guided mental imagery recordings I created.

Mindfulness During Daily Activities

When an athlete is totally engaged in his or her sport, to the exclusion of all other thoughts and stimuli, it is said that they are "in the flow." Being in the flow means being totally in the present moment, regardless of what you are doing, or whatever else is going on around you. When mindfulness teachers discuss living a mindful life, one of the more common examples is washing dishes, but it can be any activity.

Hobbies are a great example of being in the moment, such as gardening, crafts, wildlife photography or cooking. One of my favorite examples is working on a jigsaw puzzle. Consider making a list of five of your top favorite activities that you engage in, including physical exercise. If you don't have five, then write down whatever comes to mind. Next, call to mind your favorite hobby or activity outside of your employment. If you don't have a hobby, what is an activity you wish you had as a hobby (it's never too late to start, including learning a musical instrument)? Once you have identified these, shift gears and become engaged in one of these activities.

If you have the time and the weather cooperates, consider taking a mindful walk outside.

Creative Mindfulness Practices

Some of our best creative moments come during periods of stillness, when strokes of brilliance bubble to the surface of a quiet mind. An idea with some energy behind it can change your life for the better. Mindful activities that engage our sense of creativity include drawing, creating a vision board (also known as a treasure map), making a Shutterfly book of recent photos on your cell phone, and coming up with a new recipe for dinner. Ask yourself, what is your greatest creative passion? Once you have this answer the next thing to do is to act on it, and make it happen.

11

Guided Meditations

The following three guided meditations have been created to support your mindfulness journey. Simply scan the QR codes below with your smartphone to access the audio recordings, where I personally guide you through each transformative practice.

Cloud Breathing Mindfulness Practice

 This mindful breathing meditation guides you through a powerful visualization technique that transforms ordinary breathing into a cleansing and energizing practice. You'll breathe in pure white light that fills your body with fresh energy while exhaling dark clouds that carry away tension, stress, and anything that no longer serves you, ultimately leaving you feeling restored, centered, and equipped with a valuable tool for maintaining calm awareness throughout your day.

Mindful Body Scan

 This mindful body scan meditation systematically guides you on a journey of awareness from head to toe, teaching you to notice physical sensations, release tension, and cultivate a deep sense of present-moment connection with your body. Beginning with breath awareness and

grounding, you'll learn to direct gentle attention to each part of your body—arms, legs, torso, and face—observing sensations with curiosity rather than judgment, ultimately integrating this awareness into a unified sense of wholeness and calm that you can carry into your daily activities.

Waves of Peace

 This guided beach visualization takes you on an inner journey to a tranquil shoreline at sunrise, where the rhythmic sound of waves becomes synchronized with your breathing to wash away tension and concerns. Using the ocean as a powerful metaphor for inner peace, this meditation helps you experience profound spaciousness and calm, teaching you to let the natural rhythm of waves reshape your inner landscape and leave you feeling deeply rejuvenated and centered.

12

Mindful Nature Breaks

Sometimes the most effective meditation happens when we connect with the natural world. The following collection of short nature videos, personally recorded by me at beautiful locations around the world, offers you a chance to step away from daily stressors and immerse yourself in peaceful outdoor settings. Whether you use these scenes as a meditation focal point, a breathing exercise backdrop, or simply a moment of calm in your day, let nature's rhythm guide you toward greater stillness and presence.

These videos work beautifully as:

- a starting point for meditation practice
- a calming transition between stressful activities
- a mindful break during your workday
- background ambiance for breathing exercises

Find a comfortable position, take a deep breath, and allow these natural moments to support your journey toward inner peace.

Snow Falling on Cherry Blossoms

Pink Thunderhead Clouds & Crickets

Assaranca Waterfall, County Donegal, Ireland

Ocean Surf, Kauai, Hawaii

Appendix A

Establishing and Engaging in Healthy Boundaries

*"When we fail to set boundaries and hold people
accountable, we feel used and mistreated."*
—Brené Brown

It is impossible to talk about meditation without doing a deeper dive into the topic of healthy boundaries. Simply stated, healthy boundaries are positive behaviors that promote balance and integrity in our lives. Moreover, they are behavioral "guardrails" that promote wellbeing. Sometimes good boundaries mean "No!" or "Do not enter/invade my space." Other times they underscore the importance of the expression: "Everything in moderation," particularly with eating habits. Healthy boundaries are assertiveness in action. Some people call them a series of minor "course corrections" to help navigate life without become shipwrecked. In essence, good boundaries are appropriate behaviors for optimal living. This, however, is easier said than done!

All aspects of our lives require some sense of healthy boundaries, whether it's finances, eating habits, alcohol consumption, sleep habits, technology habits, or even relationships. Some boundaries are common sense. Others require trial and error, and refinement for our ever-changing circumstances. With many personal boundaries, having a sense of flexibility is essential! Boundaries without flexibility lead to rigidity, unhappiness, and perhaps even dogma. Balance is the key, yet this type of balance takes lots of practice, discipline, will power and refinement.

As young children, we first learn healthy behaviors (basic do's and dont's) from our parents, grandparents and teachers, to help us avoid danger and keep some sense of organization in the social structure. Classic examples may include the following: "Don't put your hand on the hot stove.""No phone calls after 9:00 pm.""Cover your mouth when you sneeze." "In bed by 9:00 pm," or "No cell phones at the dinner table." Without boundaries in place, parents will get walked over. Children, on the other hand, often despise rules and healthy boundaries. They want complete freedom, which can result in pushing the edge of the boundaries to exhaustion. Everyone loves freedom, however, freedom without responsibility can lead to pure chaos. Healthy boundaries help ensure a sense of moral stability.

People who don't have healthy boundaries often feel like doormats that everyone walks on. I call it the amoeba syndrome. The repercussions of poor boundaries include feelings of resentment and victimization by others, and at times, even by oneself. Over time, feelings of victimization can certainly foster a sense of anxiety. Without healthy boundaries, these feelings can eventually feed upon themselves, with further behaviors that spiral into a deeper sense of uncertainty and personal chaos.

When we turn eighteen years old, many parents consider this job to be over and they no longer insist on what may have been referred to as rules of the house (e.g., When you live under this roof, you will do as I say). Once we become adults, however, we become responsible for creating and establishing specific rules or boundaries for ourselves. In a perfect world this sounds ideal, but there are various factors that disrupt this process, including laziness, apathy, fear and of course the ego, which may insist that some boundaries aren't even necessary. Often the result is that all hell breaks loose. Poor personal boundaries, however, result in feeling overwhelmed, resentful, annoyed, and victimized—all of which contribute to a critical mass of stress.

Currently, in our society, humans have a love affair with screen technology, adding yet another layer of complexity to the concept of healthy boundaries—in some cases, turning the concept on its head. It's no secret that screen addictions and FOMO (Fear of Missing Out) have resulted in car accidents, strained relationships, and poor sleep habits, ruined marriages, and modeled less than ideal behavior for our children. Today the Internet has become a public utility and has become essential for functioning in various aspects of life. Conversely, the convenience of worldwide access 24/7 has created its own set of problems, from Pavlovian responses to text messages to binge watching favorite shows through all hours of the night. Healthy boundaries with screen devices (from the phone to the TV) may include a media curfew (no screen devices an hour before bedtime). It may also include abstaining from doom-scrolling, limited time on social media and avoiding fear-based headline click-bait.

When initiating a meditation practice, it is essential to communicate to those you live with your need for them to respect your quiet time and not interrupt, distract or disturb your meditation time. Remind friends and family to honor your quiet time. If they don't have a meditation practice, they may not understand, so you may have to remind them repeatedly. It can require courage to assert your boundaries so that your personal rules are not violated. Meditation itself requires a few healthy boundaries to get started. For example, honor your own needs by leaving your screen device outside the meditation room so that it doesn't become a distraction. In a short period of time, meditation helps regulate the boundaries of our emotions so that they don't control us and make us victims of our anger or fear.

We can all use an occasional course correction in our lives. This is why New Year's Eve resolutions are made and behavior modification rituals exist. Are there any areas in your life that could use a course correction? There is no time like the present.

Appendix B

Selected Essays by
Brian Luke Seaward
from the WINN Journal

Still the Mind, Fill the Heart

You must remain very still to get a hummingbird to perch on your hand as you hold a small bowl of sweet nectar in your palm. The slightest movement signals these tiny birds that it is not safe to land, let alone feed. Last summer I taught my wife's grandson how to be still and attract hummingbirds. What looked like a lesson in communing with nature was really a lesson in stillness.

I explained that not only did he have to keep his arm and hand as still as a statue, it was essential for him to send love from his heart up through his shoulder, down his arm and through his hand, so the birds would sense his good intentions. Many people who try to do this try too hard, become anxious, and emit a sense of tension that the birds pick up on. Being still and gently broadcasting a feeling of love from our hearts can create a field of compassion in ourselves and our surroundings. This little boy listened to every word I said, closed his eyes and mustered up enough love to attract nearly all the hummingbirds in Colorado. It worked!

For the next 30 minutes he had swarms of Broadtail, Calliope, and Rufus hummingbirds eating out of the palm of his hand, sometimes five or six at a time.

In this high-tech age of video games, social media, and binge watching, where our attention ricochets around our personal space like a thousand bouncing ping pong balls, moments of stillness are rare moments indeed. We add in smart-phone calls, text alerts, and video meetings and end up living in a culture of constant distraction. What we have gained with always-present sources of information and entertainment (we gorge on eye candy), we have lost in our ability to be calm and still. The immediate gratification of our desire for facts, fun, and ego-soothing messages is at odds with being able to concentrate, to be quietly attentive, or even to experience a sense of grace that can only be acquired through the discipline of sitting still. We have lost the ability to find balance, to achieve mental homeostasis.

What the ego sees as victory, the soul sees as stolen moments. In essence, we have lost the ability to maintain clear, conscious awareness where we can glimpse the greater reality beyond us. But we can regain this ability with the simple practice of stillness, also known as meditation. The quest for a still mind is not a recent phenomenon. It has given rise to many practices for thousands of years. Sacred texts and teachings from many traditions speak of stillness.

For example, Psalm 46 says: *Be still and know that I am God.*

Lao Tzu wrote of stillness in the *Tao Te Ching*:

To the mind that is still, the whole universe surrenders.

The Australian Aborigines have a word for stillness, *dadirri,* that means an inner listening during periods of quiet, a still awareness.

And in the *Bhagavad Gita* there is this:

Still your mind in me, still yourself in me
And without a doubt
You shall be united with me,
Lord of Love, dwelling in your heart.

Buddhist monks spend years cultivating stillness of mind to gain insight from the depths of the unconscious. This simple practice (though, not that simple) is to stop the chatter of the small self, known in the West as the ego. By calming the activity of the ego, deep-seated wisdom may surface and shed light on the nature of Being.

The stillness of the mind has been compared to many things. The most common metaphor is of the smooth surface of a mountain lake. Where there is an active ego and busy brain there are countless ripples on the lake's surface. The goal is to silence the ego's ragged rants of fear-based thinking so that the surface of the water becomes so still that it can reflect, like a mirror, all that is around it.

So, how do we reclaim the lost art of stillness? We can begin by dedicating time each day to sitting quietly, without interruption. Mornings, before breakfast, often works best. Start by finding a quiet place where there is little risk of being disturbed. Next, remove all distractions – such as cell phones or computer screens. Then, sit comfortably, close your eyes and focus on your breathing. Place all of your attention first on the inhalation (in-breath) and then the exhalation (out-breath). If your mind wanders (and it will) simply call your attention back to your breathing.

Start with five minutes of simple diaphragmatic breathing, feeling the breath enter and leave your body as you breathe in and out, paying attention either to the sensations around your nose or around your stomach as you feel the diaphragm rise and fall. After you master 5 minutes of being aware of your breath, consider adding a few minutes each day making a 30-minute duration the goal. Also, consider keeping a pad of paper and pen nearby to jot down thoughts that beg for your attention. Sometimes valuable ideas arise that will be less distracting if you write them down and then get right back to focusing on the breath.

The art of stillness is far more than physical stillness. Once you have removed external distractions, turn to internal distractions – those thoughts and emotions generated by the ego. Stillness includes keeping the mind calm and focused and this takes practice. The beauty of a still mind is that once distractions have been tamed, sensory perceptions are greatly increased, and we can experience and observe more than we ever could have imagined.

One of the first obstacles we meet on the path to stillness is the need to be busy. Whether it's a cultural influence (think the Puritan Ethic), or the constant lure of social media, we are used to always being active, always doing something or thinking about what we could be doing. And while working certainly adds a sense of purpose to our lives, wisdom keepers the world over remind us that it is in the moments of stillness that imagination, intuition, creativity, and insight reside. Before one can access these gifts, action must give way to non-action. In doing so, the ego will fight the demand to do nothing. Yet the secret is that nothing is really something – it's the essential preparation for emptiness that is required for the more subtle thought processes to reveal themselves. And that is also where we can sit with the experience of love.

Upon returning home from the mountains where the hummingbirds first greeted us with delight, my wife's grandson was eager to see if he could attract other birds to land on his hand. Patience, as it turns out, is both a requirement and a gift returned for practicing the art of stillness. I noticed how the carry-over effect of stillness lingered in other activities that this lively boy engaged in. (I have also noticed that in myself.) The next day I found him sitting ever so quietly in the backyard, arm outstretched with some sunflower seeds in the palm of his hand. Patiently waiting. Patiently practicing stillness. It took several attempts (nearly an hour), but his effort to sit still paid off. A chickadee landed on his fingertips and took a seed, then flew away. The rewards of stillness are immeasurable.

This essay first appeared in the WINN journal on February 5, 2021. Reprinted with Permission. All Rights Reserved.

Of Brain and Mind

A few years ago, I was invited to participate in a study of the effects of Cranio-Sacral Therapy on stress and relaxation. My first day in the lab I was fitted with a skull cap with countless electrodes ready to record my brain's electrical activity. Once fitted, I lay down and within seconds one of the researchers said, "Oh, you're a meditator. We can always tell who meditates the moment these electrodes are attached." Sadly, I did not find out if CST promotes relaxation since I was in the researchers' control group, but the skull cap with electrodes fascinated me. What was going on in my head?

I have been intrigued with matters of the mind and brain since I was a child. Learning about intuition, telekinesis, psychic activity, and remote viewing intrigued me when I was in high school. In college, I became particularly interested in the role our thoughts play in the stress response and perhaps more importantly, in healing chronic illness related to stress. Later, I became curious about consciousness after I discovered the work of Carl Jung. My educational training taught me that the mind is produced in the gray matter of the brain as the result of very complex (yet unexplained) brain chemistry. However, all my personal psychic experiences (combined with those reported by credible sources) showed me that the brain/mind puzzle was anything but solved, and in the west many mental phenomena were not even addressed.

Every now and then I would get excited about new findings in medicine that might provide answers, only to be disappointed. The March 2005 cover story of the *National Geographic* magazine read, "What's in Your Mind?" and displayed a photograph of a Tibetan monk with scores of electrodes covering his forehead, scalp, and face. Sadly, for anyone curious about what secrets the mind really holds, the article never did say. Instead, once again, the complete focus was on brain physiology while secrets of the mind remained unexplored.

The common assumption in Western science has been that the mind and brain are the same thing. The brain—with its hemispheres and lobes, hypothalamus, pineal gland, hippocampus and amygdala—has been dissected, weighed and, most recently, scanned repeatedly. Researchers did make the remarkable discovery that the number of brain cells is not fixed at birth. Instead, we have the ability to create new brain cells and, perhaps more importantly, to alter the existing neural wiring – a phenomenon called "neuroplasticity." And while brain and mind, like overlapping circles depicted in a Venn diagram, seem to share a sliver of common space, experts who study both confide that they indeed, are not the same thing. At best, many western-based researchers regard the mind as an "epiphenomenon" of the brain. But those who study the mind will tell you that the mind is not a by-product of brain activity although mind uses the brain as its physical basis for organization and expression.

At the beginning of the 20th century Sigmund Freud, a Western-trained physician, placed the study of unconscious thought on the medical map. Before Freud there had been little consideration of the subjective and hidden operations of the brain. Freud's student, Carl Jung, furthered our understanding of the mind with the concept of collective consciousness. There's a fascinating story that at a private luncheon where the conversation was about quantum physics, Albert Einstein explained to Jung that everything is energy and this led Jung to conceptualize the collective unconscious. Later after decades of research, Wilder Penfield stated as well that although the brain was the primary organ for the mind, consciousness existed outside of the brain. Researcher Candace Pert came to the same conclusion stating:

"I think it is now possible to conceive of mind and consciousness as an emanation of emotional processing and as such, mind and consciousness would appear to be independent of brain and body."

Over the course of my career as a health psychologist, I have had the great pleasure to meet many innovative thinkers including Elmer Green, Larry Dossey, Richard Gerber, Candace Pert as well as others who were also trying to gain a better understanding of what the mind really is and how it really works.

Elmer Green, Ph.D. is considered the founder of clinical biofeedback. Working at the Menninger Foundation with his wife Alyce, he taught people how to self-regulate physical processes such as blood pressure or heart rate. Although biofeedback is a body-based system, the Green's goal was to teach people how to master emotional responses so they could calm and clear their minds and go on to achieve higher states of consciousness.

At about the same time that researchers were placing electrodes on Tibetan monks' heads or running Functional MRI tests to gain a better understanding of brain physiology and, they thought, its link to the mind, a group of maverick research pioneers continued to work to better understand the relationship between the material brain and the non-material mind. What had begun in the 1970s as mind-body medicine later became mind-body-spirit approaches to human health and well-being. Here are some of the pioneering researchers, doctors, physicists, and parapsychologists whose work and writing taught me much that I have wanted to know about consciousness, parapsychology, subtle energies, healing, and enlightened states of mind.

Larry Dossey, M.D., physician and author of books containing empirical studies of prayer, non-local healing, and the powers of conscious thought and intention. (Like Elmer, Larry's credibility opened the way for me to explore these phenomena.)

Charles Tart, Ph.D., one of the founders of the field of transpersonal psychology devoted his career to the legitimacy of parapsychology and non-local consciousness.

Stan Groff, Ph.D., pioneering researcher of the effects of psychotropic drugs on our ability to gain an expanded awareness of the nature of reality.

Raymond Moody, M.D., was the first to collect and document the experiences of people who had Near Death Experiences (NDEs).

Russell Targ, Ph.D., with Hal Puthoff, was an early developer of the remote viewing program supported by the Department of Defense.

Beverly Rubik, Ph.D., researcher who developed the field of frontier science and studied the subtle energies of living systems and spiritual healing.

Dean Radin, Ph.D., director of far-reaching research at the Institute of Noetic Sciences (IONS) and an early proponent of entanglement theory which studied the effect of conscious thought on all aspects of research.

Lynn McTaggart, health reporter and author of The Field in which she outlined countless empirical, evidence-based studies that showed the effects of conscious intention on a wide range of health outcomes.

Itzak Bentov, Ph.D., a physicist who determined that conscious thought is indeed energy and the human being is comprised of layers of energy, several of which exist outside the body.

Richard Gerber, M.D., a radiologist intrigued by the concept of Kirlian photography who wrote *Vibrational Medicine*, a classic textbook of subtle energies and energy healing.

Bruce Lipton, Ph.D., a cell biologist and one of the early advocates of epigenetics that can link consciousness (and unconscious thoughts) to the health or detriment of all cells in the human body.

Joe Dispenza, DC, an explorer of mind-body-spirit phenomena and the positive effects of conscious intention on healing systems.

Currently, the investigations into the mind and its connection to brain physiology continue. Two things are needed for standard science to advance its understanding: a greater acceptance of the solid, empirical data that has already been collected, and most importantly, a vanquishing of the fixed Western belief that the brain alone produces the mind.

My experience with the skull cap and electrodes revealed that my meditator's mind showed up as alpha brainwaves, the hallmark of a relaxed brain which I was told had become quite uncommon in this crazy, stressed-out world. That experience only validated my meditation practice and my thirst for further explorations.

If you would like to read more about the mind and consciousness, there are many good books – these are just four authors I have especially appreciated:

Larry Dossey, *One Mind*, Hay House, Carlsbad, CA, 2014.

Wilder Penfield, *Mystery of the Mind: A Critical Study of Consciousness and the Human Brain*, 2015.

Candace Pert, *Molecules of Emotion*, Scribner, New York 1997.

Raymond Moody, and Paul Perry, *Proof of Life After Death*, Atria Books, 2023. Dr Moody has written many books about the Near Death Experience and this is the first one in which he has been willing to use the word "proof."

This essay was first published in the WINN journal on January 26, 2024. Reprinted With Permission. All rights reserved.

Reflections on Coherence in Action

During the summer of 1993, a remarkable experiment took place in Washington, D.C. In an effort to help reduce crime in the nation's capital, a group of 4,000 city residents who regularly practice meditation (specifically Transcendental Meditation) were invited to create an atmosphere of tranquility over the city for a six-week period. Crime rate statistics were monitored both before and afterwards. It was observed that by the end of the experiment, the crime rate had decreased dramatically, by 48%. While this unique approach to crime reduction didn't make significant national news headlines, people who study consciousness paid attention. The name of the study was called "The National Demonstration Project to Reduce Violent Crime and Improve Government Effectiveness." The result was nicknamed "The Maharishi Effect" (after the founder of the TM movement, Maharishi Mahesh Yogi). Unofficially, the name was "The Coherence Study," and it helped shed new light on the study of consciousness, relaxation, and the relationship between the mind and quantum physics, collective energy fields, and what scientist Rupert Sheldrake referred to as "morphogenic fields."

The word coherence literally means "to stick together." It has become a term used to describe the quality of a unified whole. From a quantum physics perspective, the term "coherence" refers to the creation of a field when energies or oscillations entrain together or sync up to create an energetic field of oneness. Quantum physics speaks in terms of energy, and the results of this study suggested that consciousness is indeed, a form of energy.

People often use the word "coherent" when describing a clearly expressed idea or combination of ideas, just as the word "incoherent" is used to convey a communication is unintelligible or scrambled. People who regularly practice meditation often describe a sense of calm in their thoughts and perceptions. Brainwave measurements (EEGs) of meditators reveal that there is a balance between the left and right cerebral hemispheres, suggesting an experience of oneness in thought, or coherence. Research studies by Professor Richard Davidson and his colleagues who investigated the brain function of Tibetan monks using fMRI while they were meditating revealed the ability of the brain's neural synapses to rewire themselves in what has now become known as "neuroplasticity." Neuroplasticity, however, is not just for Tibetan monks. Anyone can reap the benefits of this kind of meditation.

Conversely, dissonance – the opposite of coherence – is revealed in a lack of harmonic vibrations. Cognitive dissonance is a term used to describe someone whose thoughts are scattered and whose behavior often exhibits behaviors influenced by stress. (The term cognitive dissonance is also used to describe behaviors that don't align with a person's values or beliefs.)

What effect does coherence have on one's health? Researchers at the HeartMath Institute have been investigating the relationship between the heart and brain to better understand the coherence between emotions and thoughts. Perhaps it's no surprise that results reveal that when our thoughts are heart-centered, arising from a place of compassion, there is greater coherence between the energetic frequencies of the heart and brain. Then too, stress-based thoughts are observed to be in dissonance with one's heart rhythms and coherence between heart and brain are compromised.

The HeartMath Institute states: "HeartMath Institute research has demonstrated that different patterns of heart activity (which accompany different emotional states) have distinct effects on cognitive and emotional function. During stress and negative emotions, when the heart rhythm pattern is erratic and disordered, the corresponding pattern of neural signals traveling from the heart to the brain inhibits higher cognitive functions. This limits our ability to think clearly, remember, learn, reason, and make effective decisions."

The HeartMath Institute is not alone in this view of consciousness. The remarkable work of Dr. Joe Dispenza also suggests the importance of coherence between our cognitive thought processes and our emotional states, with regard to physical health and healing. In his popular books, You Are the Placebo, and Becoming Supernatural, Dispenza explains the importance of creating new neural pathways (neuroplasticity) in the brain that allows for a deeper state of coherence that then allows for healing to occur through the layers of the human energy fields and energy centers (chakras). While acknowledging stress, grief and emotional pain is important, being stuck in these emotional states creates neural pathways that inhibit the healing process; also a form of dissonance.

Can our thoughts and intentions affect the greater good? The answer appears to be yes! From a larger perspective of group consciousness, it is easy to see what effect repeated, fear-based headlines and news broadcast have on society. It creates a sense of cognitive distortion, social unease and mental/emotional exhaustion. Experts in the field of stress management, specifically, Positive Psychology, often encourage people to dramatically decrease how much attention they pay to the news, particularly if they are following social media where doom-scrolling has become the norm. What is the best way to use coherence in our own lives so we can benefit planetary healing? Perhaps the best way is to maintain a robust meditation practice and end your meditations with some form of loving kindness that reaches out to the entire world. As more and more people engage in a regular meditative practice, then like the meditators in Washington D.C. we could add to the collective energies of peace and harmony on the planet in these times of dramatic change.

This essay first appeared in the WINN journal on October 9, 2024. Reprinted with Permission. All Rights Reserved.

Appendix C

Additional Tools in
Your Resiliency Toolkit

Meditation is a great tool to have in your resiliency toolkit, yet there are many others that can help build a solid foundation for your personal resiliency. Below are twenty-four additional tools (skills) to consider using when the situation calls for additional resources. They are easy to use and implement. What do these have in common with mindfulness? Each skill invites you to be in the moment. In fact, you may already be doing some of these. Remember, just like meditation and mindfulness practices, the more you practice these skills, the better they will serve you.

Find the People Doing Good

Fred Rogers, known to many as Mr. Rogers, the host of a popular PBS children's show, shared with his television audience a great idea that his mom once gave him. During a national crisis, national calamity or even a moment of personal strife, look for people doing good, and there are always people doing good. Look for people helping others in times of need. They can be found donating blood, working in food shelters, donating clothes to homeless shelters, volunteer firefighting, taking the elderly to the hospital, feeding the hungry or perhaps random acts of kindness like opening a door for someone, or "giving cuts" in the grocery store. Even in a world of strife, there are always people doing good. Most likely, you won't see them on the news, but they are there. Search them out. And where possible follow in their footsteps. Helping others is one of the best ways to make the world a better place!

Body Hacks for Relaxation: 4-7-8 Breathing Exercise

There are countless ways to initiate the relaxation response through diaphragmatic breathing. One method made popular by Andy Weil, MD is the 4-7-8 Breathing Technique. It is very simple. It has 4 steps that you repeat for 1-2 minutes... Step 1: Exhale to empty your lungs of air as best you can. Step 2: Inhale slowly and quietly through your nose for a count of 4 seconds. Step 3: Hold your breath for 7 seconds. Step 4: Exhale forcefully through your mouth (making a "whoosh" sound through your lips) for 8 seconds. Repeat for 4 breath cycles. Dr. Weil suggests practicing this every day, twice a day, and noticing the calming effect it produces.

Unplug from Social Media for 1 Hour Each Day

Doom scrolling, social comparisons, approval seeking (with likes and comments)—social media plays with our emotions and hits us where we are most vulnerable. It may be unrealistic to unplug completely from Twitter, Facebook, Snapchat, Instagram, TikTok, YouTube, and others, but staying plugged in all the time is like pouring gasoline on the fire of stress.

Adopt an Attitude of Gratitude

Yes, life can have its horrible moments, and when those occur, take time to grieve. But life has many awesome moments too. We take so much for granted. An attitude of gratitude isn't proposing rainbows and unicorns. It simply offers some balance in a crazy world. Name three things you are grateful for. Even horrible moments can have their silver linings.

Engage Your Vagal Tone

Activating the vagus nerve (the relaxation nerve in the body) helps intercept the stress response and calm the body. Try this:

Close your eyes and take a slow deep belly breath. Repeat. After several slow deep breaths, sense how your body feels. Humming also activates the vagus nerve. Try humming a few bars of your favorite song.

Resetting the Stress Response

It has long been known that immediately after an animal survives a threat or attack, it will physically shake its entire body. It is thought that animals do this to reset their nervous system, for they cannot maintain a heightened state of stress indefinitely. They must return to a sense of calm, foraging for food, or resting, etc. We can learn a lesson from this. Try it. Stand up and shake your body. Initiate a coordinated shaking motion from your head, shoulders and hips for a few seconds. Then sit down and relax. Note how your body feels. Try this a few times throughout the day. Shake your stress away!

Store a Tactile Keepsake Nearby

Having something to touch or grasp to engage the tactile sense has proven to be a great stress management tool when you get upset, nervous or even overwhelmed. Some people use polished gemstones (also known as tumble stones). Others hold seashells. Some people fill a small balloon with sand, seal it up and squeeze it for a moment of comfort. It doesn't matter what the object is, as long as it's something you like and find comforting to hold. Holding this item could also be a reminder of a special person or place that rekindles fond memories.

Deactivate Your Emotional Triggers

Everyone has buttons (triggers) that, when pushed, cause fear, anger, frustration and anxiety. Triggers can be all kinds of stimuli, including people, places, situations, etc. Before you can deactivate your triggers, you first must know what they are. Make a short list. Then make it a point to ask yourself why do these stressors elicit such a response? The path of least resistance may work for some, but avoidance is an ineffective coping technique. Time to let go and move on.

Know What You Can (and Cannot) Control

Control is thought to be an illusion. There is little in life that we can control, except our own emotions. We cannot control the stock market, the weather, or even other people. Yet people do spend a lot of energy trying to have power over those things they will never control. Like spinning the back wheels of a car in a muddy ditch, nothing will happen. You can control your thoughts and emotions, but even this takes practice. Make a daily habit of asking yourself, "Am I trying to take charge of something that is impossible to control?" When the answer is yes, let it go and move on.

Choose Love Over Fear

When you find yourself getting upset over something (e.g., anxious, cynical, sarcastic, rude, annoyed, etc.), observe your behavior, including your thoughts. Are you acting out of fear? Fear is the easiest default behavior to act upon. Moreover, it becomes addictive and tends to generate more fear-based thoughts. You have a choice. Fear or love/compassion. At first it takes effort not to fall into the fear mindset. Each time you do it you become better at it. Choose love/compassion over fear; the rewards are exponentially better.

Read Inspirational Quotes

Quotes from Nelson Mandela, Anne Morrow Lindberg, Carl Jung, Maya Angelou, Mary Oliver or Brené Brown can really raise your spirits and offer a valuable course correction in your day to avoid becoming spiritually shipwrecked. Find a quote you like, post it close by, and read it often. Let the wisdom in the message lift your spirits. If you don't have one on hand, search online for "inspirational quotes"—you will have plenty to choose from. Or search for a quote from your favorite hero or mentor. Here are two examples:

"Tension is who you think you should be. Relaxation is who you are."

– Chinese proverb

"Keep some room in your heart for the unimaginable."

– Mary Oliver

Reframe the Current Situation

While stressors are very real, people tend to make mountains out of mole hills. Moreover, with stress, there can be a lot of personal victimization. There is a proverb that states: Each situation has a good side and a bad side; each moment you decide. So, you can be a prisoner of your thoughts or a master; the choice is yours. Identify a stressor right now and without being cynical, reframe the situation to see a different and more positive perspective.

Step Back and See the Big Picture!

Many stressors seem like either personal attacks or insurmountable problems. Learn to step back from the situation to see the bigger picture. When you do this, quite often it becomes obvious that it was neither personal nor insurmountable. Something to ask yourself as you step back is this: Will this even matter a year from now?

Try Doodling to Relax

When you get stressed or frustrated, grab a pen, pencil or any writing utensil and doodle on a blank piece of paper. If you have some colored pens, even better. Start with some curves, perhaps a few circles, or even some lines, maybe a face or a smile. Doodling anything can ease your mind and shift your mindset from a left brain (judgmental) to a right brain (acceptance) thought process. Doodling is a great example of being in the moment.

Take Your Daily Dose of Vitamin H (Humor)

Humor may be in short supply when you are stressed, but there is always something to laugh or smile about (how many times have you said to yourself, "A year from now this will be funny." Life is filled with irony and incongruities. Self-deprecating humor takes the sting out of a bad situation. Self-deprecating humor is also the best form of humor (making fun of yourself without deflating your self-esteem). Cartoons, jokes and short videos are only a keystroke away. Find something humorous to laugh at once a day (including yourself) and more funny things will start coming your way.

Create and Use Your Own Personal Sanctuary

Everyone needs a place to call their own. It can be as simple as a corner of some room where you can sit with your back up against the wall, close your eyes, and still the mind. The need for a personal sanctuary is timeless and spans every culture and corner of the world. Some people call this a sacred space. While some personal sanctuaries may resemble palace gardens, all you really need is a quiet place to call your own (this does not include the bathroom toilet). Having a designated place helps when you need to get away from the world's madness. And while it can include a pillow to sit on, a book to read, and even a cup of hot tea, all you need is some small place to call your own. Once you have created it, then make it a habit to enjoy it regularly.

Reach Out to a Friend

One cure for isolation is to reach out to a friend and strengthen your bond of humanity. Bond with a friend over a cup of coffee or tea where you can unload your troubles, cry on a metaphorical shoulder or seek validation where necessary. Text, zoom, email, or call, but reach out. Remember, in a highly virtual world in which we live, in-person contact is the best. If friends are in short supply, family works too (so do pets). Support groups are an asset as well. And the benefits of reaching out are two-fold. You benefit, but so does the person whom you reached out to. Often, they need the social contact as much, if not more than you. Reach out now!

Give Thanks

Take a moment and give thanks for all that is going right for you. Practicing an attitude of gratitude is one of the best ways to reset the mind and cancel the victim attitude that becomes so prevalent when things are not going as planned. It also helps put things in perspective. Do you have a roof over your head? Give thanks. Do you have a pair of shoes? Give thanks. Can you breathe without a respirator? Give thanks. There are countless things to be grateful for, most commonly the things we take for granted until we don't have them anymore. So take a moment to give thanks.

Create and Use a Personal Mantra

Repeat one of the following phrases to yourself, as you exhale, for the next five to ten breaths: "I am safe." "I am calm and relaxed." "I release that which I cannot control." "I will respond, rather than react to situations today."

Repeat your favorite mantra several times throughout the day.

Invoke the 5 x 5 Rule

Are you stressed about something? Does it make you angry or upset, anxious or afraid? If so, invoke the 5 x 5 rule. As yourself this: Is this issue, problem, or concern going to matter in 5 years? Most likely not! Perhaps it won't even matter in 1 year. Most likely not even a month from now. So if it won't matter in 5 years, don't spend more than 5 minutes being upset about it. Grieve now and let it go. Don't waste the emotional energy, nor the mental energy for something that will be very insignificant down the road. Remember the sage advice from Mark Twain: "I'm an old man now, and I have known a great many problems, most of which never happened."

Picture This!

Identify a favorite nature scene that you find to be really relaxing. Perhaps a beach scene, a cathedral forest, or an image of the Teton Mountain Range. Find a picture or photo of that scene and tape it to your computer screen, bathroom mirror, fridge or someplace where you can see it frequently. When you get stressed, upset, or flummoxed, let your mind wander to this place as a personal refuge of relaxation. You can have more than one too.

Surround Yourself with Beauty

No doubt there is a lot of ugliness in the world today. All one needs to do is listen to the news to validate this fact. But you can balance the score with positive sensory stimuli. Surround yourself with beauty! There is beauty in nature, beauty in art work, beauty in poetry, beauty in greenhouses. If you take the time to look, there is beauty just about everywhere. Where do you choose to place your attention? Take a moment or two to surround yourself in beauty today.

Seek Out Pleasant Smells, Aromas and Fragrances

If you are flooded with stressful thoughts, consider replacing stressful stimuli with something pleasant, even if only for a few minutes, to gain some mental clarity. The scent of fresh roses, the aroma of freshly ground coffee beans, the smell of freshly baked bread. Balsam pine fur. Earl Gray tea. Keep something on your desk that you can grab and wave past your nostrils long enough to unplug from the world of stress and regain your composure. The term is aromatherapy, but a rose by any other name smells equally nice.

Get Centered

Getting stuck in your head and carrying the weight of the world on your shoulders is an unbearable load to carry. Take a slow, deep breath and focus your attention on the center of your body (an inch or two below your belly button). Stand up and feel your body's center. Feel how this differs from being "top heavy" with thoughts that weigh you down. Once centered, you are in a better position to think clearly. Give it a try now.

Appendix D

Loving-Kindness Meditation

This meditation exercise uses words, images, and feelings to evoke the intention of loving-kindness and friendliness toward oneself and others. Please keep in mind that there are many versions of this exercise, some with different nuances, wording and phrases, yet the intention is the same. Please feel free to adapt these phrases to create a way that is most meaningful for you.

With each recitation of the phrases, you are expressing a specific intention, planting the seeds of loving wishes, over and over in your heart. With a loving heart as the background, all that we attempt, all that we encounter will open and flow more easily. You can begin this practice of loving-kindness by meditating for fifteen or twenty minutes in a quiet place, your own sacred space. Let yourself sit in a comfortable fashion. Let your body rest and be relaxed. Let your heart be soft. Let go of any plans or preoccupations of the mind including any distractions.

Begin with the focus on yourself. Breathe gently and recite the first set of phrases silently to yourself, inwardly, focusing these traditional phrases directly toward your own well-being. Take a slow deep breath after each affirmation. You begin with yourself because without loving yourself it is difficult to love others. Then follow the first set of phrases with the second set that moves from the individual to the world. Again, take a slow deep breath after each affirmation. It is suggested to slowly repeat this cycle of phrases two to three times.

May I be filled with loving-kindness.

May I be filled with happiness, health and wellbeing.

May I be safe from inner and outer conflicts, pain and harm.

May I be well in mind, body and spirit, and awakened fully.

May I be at ease, happy and live a life of good health.

May I give and receive gratitude and appreciation for this day.

• • •

May your life be filled with loving-kindness.

May you be filled with happiness, health and wellbeing.

May you be safe from inner and outer conflicts, pain and harm.

May you be well in mind, body and spirit and awakened fully.

May you be at ease, happy and live a life of good health.

May you acknowledge and receive gratitude and appreciation for this day.

Appendix E

Study Guide Questions

These study guide questions are designed to help you process and integrate the concepts from *Mind Over Anxiety* into your daily life. Some questions focus on specific information, while others invite deeper reflection and personal connection. You can work through these individually for personal growth or use them as discussion starters in book clubs or study groups.

Core Concepts & Understanding

1. In what specific ways does stress influence your thought patterns throughout a typical day? Can you identify particular triggers or times when this is most noticeable?

2. What was most surprising to you about learning how stress and meditation can physically change brain structure and function? How does this knowledge change your perspective on mental health?

3. How would you explain the distinction between the mind and the brain to someone unfamiliar with this concept? What role does each play in your experience of anxiety?

4. What specific behaviors or habits could you adopt to support your brain health? Which ones feel most achievable for you right now?

5. Meditation Practice & Application

6. Based on your reading and experience, how would you define meditation to someone who has never tried it?

7. What obstacles or frustrations have you encountered (or do you anticipate) when trying to establish a consistent meditation practice? How might you address these challenges?

8. Explain the "Three Rs" of meditation and how each component contributes to an effective practice.

9. Why are healthy boundaries essential for developing and maintaining a meditation routine? What boundaries might you need to set in your own life?

10. After exploring different meditation styles—including breathing techniques and mental imagery—which approaches resonate most with you? What makes certain techniques more appealing or effective for your needs?

Integration with Daily Life

1. Given how technology and modern society often discourage stillness and quiet reflection, what strategies do you use (or could you develop) to cultivate moments of calm in your daily routine?

2. Since beginning your meditation practice, what changes have you observed in your physical health, mental clarity, emotional regulation, or overall well-being?

3. What new coping strategies and resilience tools have you added to your mental health toolkit through this journey?

4. How can you apply mindfulness principles to routine activities like eating, walking, or working?

5. What environmental changes in your home or workspace could better support your mental wellness goals?

6. What is the most significant insight or takeaway from this book that you want to carry forward in your life?

Appendix F

Meditation Books

Below is a list of books that I keep in my meditation room and that I frequently use to conclude each meditation session. I do this by reading a suggested passage, then sitting still afterward for a few moments and contemplate how I can embody this message in the course of my day.

365 Tao: Daily Meditations, Deng Ming-Dao

Opening Doors Within, Eileen Caddy

Prayers for Healing, Maggie Oman (ed)

Yes, And…:Daily Meditations, Richard Rohr

Courage to Change: One Day at a Time in Al-Alon II, Al-Anon Family Groups

Reflections in the Light: Daily Thoughts and Affirmations, Shakti Gawain

To Bless the Space Between Us, John O'Donohue

Earth Medicine: Ancestors Ways of Harmony for Many Moons, Jamie Sams

The Celtic Spirit: Daily Meditations for the Turning Year, Caitlin Matthews

Metaphysical Meditations, Paramahansa Yogananda

Tao Te Ching, Lao Tzu

The Prophet, Kahlil Gibran

The Promise of a New Day: A Book of Daily Meditations, Hazelden Meditation Series

The Woman's Book of Courage, Sue Patton Thoele

Pocketful of Miracles, Joan Borysenko, Ph.D.

The Soul of the World: A Modern Book of Hours, Phil Cousineau and Eric Lawton

365 Zen: Daily Readings, Jean Smith (ed)

365 Health and Happiness Boosters, M. J. Ryan

365 Days of Love, Daphne Rose Kingma

Life Prayers, Elizabeth Roberts and Elias Amidon

Earth Prayers, Elizabeth Roberts and Elias Amidon

The Tao of Healing, Haven Trevino

Acknowledgments

Special thanks to my editor and publisher, Lisa Duff, for bringing this much-needed book into the world. Your insight, wisdom and tremendous effort are nothing less than brilliant. Special thanks to Connie Shaw for your editorial acumen in making these words flow so beautifully on the page. With gratitude to my wife, Chris, who smiles whenever I practice mindfulness meditation in our backyard garden, watching the hummingbirds. Heartfelt gratitude to my good friends Mark Johnson, Mark Lersch and Connie Clancy for their helpful feedback, as well. I am forever indebted to the giants of consciousness research including Larry Dossey, MD; Elmer Green; Deepak Chopra; Beverly Rubik and the wonderful people at the Noetic Sciences Institute. A very special thank you to all my former college students, Olympic athletes, corporate executives, and scores of my Fall Mountain Retreat participants, who helped me hone my teaching skills to share this wisdom of mind over anxiety with the world.

About the Author

Brian Luke Seaward, Ph.D., a leading voice in stress management and wellness, has been helping people find their calm in life's storms for over four decades. As the head of the Paramount Wellness Institute in Boulder, Colorado, he's much sought after by major organizations like Wells Fargo, HP, Procter & Gamble and the U.S. military when they want to help their staff deal with stress and find better work-life balance.

With a fascinating blend of exercise physiology, environmental health, and psychology in his academic toolkit, Dr. Seaward brings a unique perspective to understanding how we can live healthier, more balanced lives. He's not just another stress management guru—he's someone who truly understands how our minds, bodies, and spirits work together.

If you've picked up a book on stress management at your university, there's a good chance it was Brian's textbook, *Managing Stress: Principles and Strategies for Health and Well-Being*. Now in its eleventh edition, it's become the gold standard for teaching stress management in colleges worldwide. He's written twenty other books, including the inspiring and best-selling *Stand Like Mountain, Flow Like Water*.

When he's not writing or teaching, you might catch Dr. Seaward sharing his wisdom in *Prevention* Magazine, *The Huffington Post*, or *The Wall Street Journal*. He's also created some eye-opening documentaries about stress management and healing—because sometimes we all need a little visual reminder of what matters most in life.

What sets Dr. Seaward apart is his down-to-earth approach to wellness. Whether he's speaking to corporate executives, healthcare workers, Olympic athletes, college students, or mountain retreat participants, his message remains the same: in today's fast-paced world, taking care of ourselves isn't just important—it's essential.

More from Wetware Media on Audio

Take us with you—whether you're driving, walking, or relaxing. Explore Wetware Media's catalog of top-selling self-improvement audiobooks.

Scan the code below with your phone to browse our complete catalog on Audible.com.